The Tenderfoot Comes West

The Tenderfoot Comes West

Half a Century of Progress
in California,
and the Petroleum Industry

by Roy P. McLaughlin

An Exposition-Lochinvar Book

EXPOSITION PRESS   NEW YORK

EXPOSITION PRESS INC.

386 Park Avenue South   New York, N.Y. 10016

FIRST EDITION

LIBRARY OF CONGRESS CATALOGUE-CARD NUMBER 68-16646

EP 46765

To

MY MOTHER *and* MY WIFE

and all pioneer women who brought culture to the far West

Foreword

HERE IS a personal chronicle. It combines family background and the experience of the author; in so doing, it spans more than a century of time. It relates accounts of life on the frontier and in California after the Gold Rush, and so sets the stage for the unfolding of the author's own life and his interestingly varied and successful career. It is, in fact, a *memoir*, well seasoned with anecdotes and reminiscences of people and places, and of the progressive efforts of men during the past half-century and more to discover, use and regulate the wealth of nature which lies on and beneath the surface earth of California and nearby states.

Chronicles such as this supply the historian with both fact and the feel of life and times. As an erstwhile historian, and as president of Roy McLaughlin's alma mater, I thank him for *The Tenderfoot Comes West* and for the opportunity to express my thanks and congratulations in this brief Foreword.

J. E. WALLACE STERLING
President, Stanford University

Stanford, California
4 December 1967

Preface

I HAVE WRITTEN this book in response to the suggestions of many friends who are engaged in one of California's most important industries, the production of petroleum. They particularly wanted to know how it came about that California in 1915 enacted a unique law for the conservation of its oil and gas resources. I played an active role in obtaining that law and in its administration for several years afterward, and the subject is fully covered here. That piece of legislation, however, was only one of many others of unique character that were passed at the time of a bloodless political revolution in California. Most of those laws were far ahead of their time and have survived the test of experience.

Political commentators and writers are often at a loss to understand Californians' political behavior. Some of them refer to us as mavericks, that is, unbranded critters on the open range. By the same token they brand themselves tenderfeet, that is, persons who do not understand the Old West.

With the purpose of making this book interesting to many other Californians and possibly other readers, I have chosen to relate the facts as I actually observed them. Such a course may seem to tend toward merely personal experiences having no relation to the general subject; however, any obstacles and hardships I may have endured in my early years were by no means unusual.

California has a unique history, different from that of any other state. When the first white settlers came in from Mexico, they soon lost contact with the Mexican government because of the vast distances and the deserts that separated them from the

City of Mexico, and they considered themselves *Californios*. Later, when Americans entered California either as mountain men engaged in the fur trade or as masters of American sailing vessels, they were far removed from the United States, and they too soon became *Californios*.

Shortly after California was admitted to the Union as a state, on September 9, 1850, without having served an apprenticeship as a territory, gold was discovered, and people rushed in from all parts of the world, some of them hardened criminals. One of the most significant events in our political history was the formation of vigilance committees in San Francisco, where corruption and crime had entirely usurped the power of government. Respectable citizens joined the committees, deported many criminals and hanged a few others. When order was restored, the committees quietly retired and returned the government to the duly elected officials. The vigilance committees are fully described by Mary F. Williams, whose father was a member of one.[1]

A second outburst of lawlessness, corruption and graft occurred in San Francisco shortly after the great earthquake and fire of 1906, and for a short time there was the threat of another vigilance committee. That was avoided, however, and the problem was solved in established courts of law. The account of what is commonly known as the graft prosecution of San Francisco is fully and interestingly described by Lately Thomas.[2] The case covered a long period of time, and the expense of the prosecution was provided by the voluntary contributions of one wealthy man.

A man named Abe Ruef was charged with being the principal intermediary in distributing bribes to governmental officials. A number of prominent men at the head of large corporations were also involved, although some of them were not convicted. The prosecuting attorney at the beginning of the trials was Francis J. Heney. When Heney was shot while in the courtroom (but not mortally wounded), his place was promptly assumed by Hiram

---

[1] *San Francisco Vigilance Committee,* "University of California Publications in History," 1921.

[2] *A Debonair Scoundrel,* 1962.

W. Johnson, who succeeded in convicting Ruef. The importance of the trial is suggested by the fact that the jury took sixty-seven days to return its verdict.

Johnson was catapulted into state politics. He was elected governor in 1910 and re-elected in 1914. He then served as United States senator until his death, on August 6, 1945. Only once was he seriously challenged in any of his campaigns for re-election to that office.[3]

Having seen a political party remain for many years under the control of an unscrupulous corporation, the people of California have enacted laws that make it difficult, *but by no means impossible,* for a political party to function.

I am indebted to Dr. W. N. Davis, Jr., Chief of Archives for the State of California for many facts; to William R. Moran of the Union Oil Company; and to Mrs. Ann Howard for the onerous task of transcribing and arranging the manuscript. The following friends have been very helpful: Josep Jensen, Edwin J. Leabow, Francis E. Minshall and Homer J. Steiney.

R. P. M.

---

[3] Herbert C. Hoover, *Memoirs,* 1951.

Contents

The Tenderfoot Comes West

CHAPTER I

Boyhood on a Ranch

IT WAS A BEAUTIFUL summer day in Colorado as I stood with my mother. Snow-flecked Mount Silver Heels made a beautiful background. People were grouped on the grassy hill between the only church in town and the stone courthouse. After a few minutes my mother led me through the gate in the rail fence and into our log-cabin home. A long time afterward I learned that the people had gathered on the hill to witness the execution of a murderer, who was to be hanged by the neck until he was dead.

Some eighty years later I stood on the same spot with my little granddaughter. The rail fence had been replaced by neat pickets, and the log cabin had been covered with boards and painted white. Otherwise, the scene appeared to have changed but little. A few old buildings had disappeared, a few new ones had been built. Of course, the livery stable, which my father had partly owned, had become a garage.

After indicating points of interest and relating some of my earliest recollections, I led my granddaughter to the courthouse to show her how justice had been dealt out in the early days. Knowing that a grown man would be courteous to a child who asked an idle question, I told her to ask the county clerk to show her the old hanging rope. He smiled, and said, "No, dearie, the rope is no longer here. It's at Mr. Smith's house." I then spoke up and said that I was born in the town. His face lit up with a broad smile. He locked the office door and led us up the narrow stairway past the room where court had never been officially adjourned. We stood at the window directly above the steps that led to the entrance of the courthouse.

As we walked away from the courthouse I told my little companion a story about a murderer, a man who shot and killed another man for the trivial offense of accidentally sprinkling water on his sidewalk. The murderer was arrested, tried and convicted, and the circuit judge sentenced him to the county jail for one year. The following evening a group of irate citizens visited the sheriff at the jail, took away his keys, locked him in a cell and escorted the prisoner to the courthouse and up the narrow stairway to the window directly above the entrance to the building. They shoved a pole out the window and hanged the murderer from it. The "posse" then visited the circuit judge, awakened him and told him what had happened and that the outgoing stage would leave at six o'clock the next morning. The judge was so prompt in arriving at the stage office that he left his baggage behind at the hotel.

My father once told me that he was glad to have been out of town that night, for it was well known that the murderer had once threatened him at the point of a gun.

The name of the town is Fairplay!

The name Fairplay was given the town by early placer miners who panned gold along the South Platte River and its tributaries. Apparently they had not been cordially received at Tarryall, a camp downstream. They dubbed that place Graball and moved upstream. The names of mining camps throughout the West reflect the humorous and carefree spirit of the young men who endured hardships in the hope that they would strike it rich. Grub Gulch, You Bet, Rough and Ready, and Harmony Ridge are a few examples.

After the early placer miners had, as they thought, scooped out all the gold from the gravel and sand along the creek, other rich deposits of both gold and silver were discovered by digging down into hard rock, and the life of the camp was prolonged for several years. Great and valuable discoveries of both silver and lead at Leadville, on the other side of the Mosquito Range, brought temporary prosperity to our town. It became a center of transportation, and many passengers were carried by stagecoach and freight from the end of the narrow-gauge railroad to the prosperous new camp.

Shortly after his discharge, on September 7, 1864, from the Union Army (my father had enlisted at the age of nineteen and served in Company I, 166th Regiment, Ohio National Guard Infantry), he, an Ohio farm boy, went to California via the Isthmus of Panama. Later he joined his brother in Colorado, where they became profitably engaged in the stagecoach and freighting business, until the building of a narrow-guage railroad along the Arkansas River to Leadville put an end to the prosperity. Our family, like many others, endured grinding poverty for several years, then finally moved away. My father retained ownership of several horses and a wagon, and with that scanty equipment he managed to support our small family. My father was the youngest of nine children. His father, after serving his apprenticeship as a weaver in his native Belfast, North Ireland, came to Ohio, bought a tract of government land, cleared it of virgin forest, and there reared his family.

For many years it was always a welcome sound when my mother said, "We are going to Grandpa's house today"—a fifteen-mile trip that meant half a day of driving to the home of Grand-father Parmelee. The last such trip stands out most clearly in my memory: I was too young to realize that we were abandoning the place of my birth.

Father would give a gentle flip to the reins, and the team would trot a short distance down the dusty main street and then slow to a walk as we turned into the narrow road that angled down the side of the gulch. During one of those short trips I saw for the first time in my life men actually engaged in mining gold, and for the first time I saw a green vegetable garden. The miners were all Chinese, working over the creek bottom that had once been sluiced and panned and finally been abandoned by the first white miners who had given the little town its name.

It was a tribute to the Chinese that they could actually make a garden flourish at an elevation of nearly two miles above sea level. Some tenderfoot is supposed to have once said that we had only two seasons in our part of Colorado: six months of early spring and six months of late fall. If anybody did make such a statement, he certainly deserved the despicable title of tenderfoot. Any old-timer will gladly tell of having stepped out from the kitchen door and looked at the thermometer, only to find that the mercury had disappeared beneath the forty-degrees-below-zero mark.

Chinese miners often followed after the original discoverers of pay dirt throughout the West, and they earned a living by working over the stream beds of California for a second time after the great gold rush there.

The last time I crossed the gulch I did so on a paved highway and a cement bridge. A glance toward what had once been the bed of the creek showed that the ground had finally been worked for the third time by dredging machinery. No trace of the creek could be seen, and the entire gulch was filled by huge ugly mounds of boulders, with no soil remaining.

The road toward Grandfather Parmelee's house ran over comparatively level ground with low rolling, wooded hills on one side, and on the other a wide expanse of beautiful green pasture land with only the tip of Pike's Peak showing on the far-distant eastern horizon. On the wide stretch of grass-covered land named South Park, through which the southern branch of the Platte River slowly winds and twists in its northerly tours, my grandfather had finally settled down. All this land is within the Louisiana Purchase. Had Grandfather been content to remain in his native Vermont, it is quite unlikely, his father having been a clergyman in a small village near the Canadian border, that he would have been able to become the owner of a small tract of land that could be called a farm. If, on the other hand, he had chosen to prolong his first year as a sailor and had continued that calling, he probably would have become the master of a sailing vessel (because he had a better-than-average education), and finally sailed around the Horn to California, where he might have become the owner of a *rancho* of a thousand acres or more. He decided, however, to stay on dry ground, push westward and earn his living by the hard work of developing the raw new country, and he finally settled on what was to be called a ranch, near Buffalo Springs. The simple change of the Spanish word *rancho* to the shorter and less charming *ranch* is an example of how we invading Anglos have mutilated many Spanish words. Almost the entire equipment of our early cowboys have Spanish names, but our pronunciation of them causes any cultured Mexican to grit his teeth in dismay. The original word for cowboy was *vaquero,* which under our influence soon gave way to *buckaroo.*

The Parmelee Ranch is still known by its original name, although none of my relatives have lived there for many years. The buildings are in as good condition as they were when erected eighty years ago.

Leaving the wilderness of Illinois, my grandfather took his bride to the site of the future Des Moines, Iowa. He erected a sawmill and built the first house in the community. My mother was the first white girl born there. He continued to deal with the Saux and Fox Indians and helped them get a higher price for their land than had been offered. Prosperity continued, especially while people were moving westward to the California gold rush in 1849; but when disappointed gold seekers returned to the East, hard times set in, and my grandfather's general-merchandising business fell off so much that he loaded his household goods and his family into a covered wagon and drove across the plains toward Colorado, where gold had recently been discovered. He built a sawmill in what is now Parmelee Gulch, near Denver, and supplied lumber to build the new city. The present scanty growth in the gulch that bears his name makes it seem almost impossible that the region could once have produced lumber. He later moved up Turkey Creek and for a time was at Black Hawk, near Central City, where my mother attended school.

Central City is one of our best-preserved mining camps. Another old camp worth a visit is Columbia in California, which is maintained as a state park in almost the identical condition in which I first saw it at the turn of the century.

Mother told me that on their trip across the plains they endured some unnecessary inconveniences and hardships. They could easily have lashed chairs onto the sides of the wagon, but without such furniture they were forced to sit on the wagon tongue at mealtime. Cooking was done over an open fire, with buffalo chips for fuel.

The first house my grandfather built in South Park was located in a broad gulch near a spring. It was partly carved into a hillside, one wall and the fireplace being of the hard rock in its original place, while the other parts of the building were of sawed boards or rough slabs. Adjoining this house were two others of later construction. In one of these buildings the marriage ceremony of my father and mother was performed by an itinerant clergyman named Father Dier, who sometimes donned snowshoes and carried mail over the mountains to secluded mining camps. He was always available to conduct religious services, and he preached almost anywhere that he could find people willing to listen—sometimes in saloon and gambling halls.

The old original house was abandoned shortly after my first visit, and I have a clear recollection of only a few events that occurred there. Once my grandfather returned with mail, and among the items received was a copy of a paper published in Denver. He waved it above his head and exclaimed, "Hurrah for Blaine!"

The most thrilling experience came one night when my mother awakened me and led me out of doors. There was a terrible clamor of roars and howls coming from the tree-covered hill on the opposite side of the gulch, about a quarter of a mile away. A bear had been trapped, and some of the men had gone over to kill it. We ate bear steaks for several days, a welcome change from the monotony of venison and pork.

The experience of that night recalled a funeral I had earlier attended in Fairplay. A man had been mauled by a bear, and even now I clearly remember passing the casket and seeing the man's face, partly covered with strips of court plaster. (Sanitary bandages or tape had not yet appeared.)

My grandfather's ancestors came from Kent and Surrey, England, and landed at New Haven, Connecticut, in 1635 on the *Elizabeth and Ann*. They founded the town of Guilford in 1639.

The Parmelee Ranch was a profitable and enduring asset and remains as a monument to the industry and business ability of my grandfather. When he first started toward the undeveloped western country, he was an employee of the American Fur Company, engaged in trading with Indians. He was successful as an Indian trader, and at the end of the first season he wrote a letter to his relatives in Vermont saying that his employers were satisfied with his services and had increased his salary to two hundred dollars a year.

Grandfather's house was the final touch in the development of the ranch. It still stands, comfortably occupied. It contained five bedrooms and a good-sized parlor with a large fireplace facing the bay window. There was a spacious kitchen and a dining table long enough to seat at least a dozen people. All the rooms had lath-and-plaster walls and ceilings. The cooking was done by my grandmother on a wood-burning stove. The wood box stood nearby and could be filled by a chute coming through the wall from a long hallway that opened into an adjoining room large enough to store wood for the entire winter season. In another room called the pantry, the milk was kept in tin pans until the cream rose to the surface, when it was skimmed off and churned. The first churn was a barrel-shaped affair with a dasher and a vertical handle. Later an improved churn was bought. It was a sort of box into which the cream was poured, and the box was revolved by a hand crank.

Most of the skimmed milk, together with the buttermilk, was fed to the hogs. My grandmother made excellent butter, and much of it found a ready market in Fairplay. My uncle drove there now and then and sold the butter at the general store run by Sam Cohen. When he returned from town, he brought with him many kinds of foodstuffs, which were stored in well-constructed bins and drawers in the pantry—sugar, flour, dried apples, beans and dried codfish. Once my grandfather returned from a visit in Vermont with a great luxury—a big box of maple-sugar bricks.

We remained at the ranch for several months while my father was in southern Colorado, where a railroad was under construction and where his horses and wagon would bring him profitable employment. He once told me that he occasionally saw an Indian mounted on a horse pointing a rifle at the workmen as if he were counting them.

A remarkable example of hardihood and thrift came late one afternoon to my grandfather's house. A slightly built Jewish peddler, with a large pack on his back, trudged up the snow-covered road and asked for food and lodging. This, of course, he received. He slept in the spare room and ate with the family. The next morning he spread open his pack and displayed his merchandise, some of which our folks bought. Finally he asked how much he owed my uncle. He was amazed when my uncle said that he owed nothing. That was the kind way travelers were treated in those days.

Of course, we had no modern plumbing, but in the hallway adjoining the kitchen there was a constantly flowing stream of spring water. The two modern-looking buildings that adjoined the old house were moved down near the new house. One became the carpenter shop and bunkhouse, and the other became a storage room. Between them was a den built to keep a bear cub, which finally grew large enough to furnish steaks for our dining table.

A large earth-covered and frost-proof cellar was near the old house. This cellar preserved enough potatoes for us until the next season came around. The vegetable garden did not produce lavishly—just a few beets and turnips, rhubarb and an occasional dish of strawberries.

Unfortunately my grandfather had only a few years to enjoy the new house. He died there at the age of seventy-two. His wife survived him by seventeen years, dying in the same house at the age of seventy-seven. They were buried in a lonely cemetery several miles to the south of the ranch.

The chief product of the ranch was hay, which was sold in Denver and elsewhere. It was also fed to the half dozen cows and the few horses and mules. The stable was built entirely of logs, stored a year's supply of fodder and provided shelter for all the livestock.

The neighboring ranch, the Sixty-three at Buffalo Springs, was so close that we could hear the barking of the dogs there. A cattle ranch, it had a well-constructed house and on the opposite side of the road a large bunkhouse and corral. The ranch was owned by the Cleveland Cattle Company, whose brand was three large C's covering almost one side of the animal. It certainly was visible at a distance, but it nearly ruined the value of the hide. The manager of the company was a one-armed veteran of the Civil War named Haver. He was a superb horseman, as was each of his children. Occasionally he brought them from Denver for summer vacation. His son, Sam, graduated from Stanford and became personnel manager for a large utility company in Los Angeles but eventually was killed by a demented employee.

I saw several roundups when the cattle belonging to the various ranches were brought in from the open range and cut out from the mixed herd for allotment to their respective owners. The roping and branding of calves was carried on in about the same manner as seen in our present-day rodeos. I once had the opportunity to become a cattleman myself when my grandfather presented me with a calf that carried his own brand, the "half-circle P." When my family moved away from the ranch, I lost track of the animal, which probably grew up, was sold, and climbed up the chute into a cattle car for the long ride to some stockyard. Many of the cattle were Texas longhorns, and more than once they charged at the buggy driven by my mother.

My mother's youngest brother, Horace, after he became a successful rancher, was always proud to tell that he had once been a cowpuncher. He was born in a cabin at Turkey Creek, but his speech was that of a Texan with whom he was associated for many years on the range. According to his stories, they must have been vigorous youngsters when they started out. They

might ride into a town like Buena Vista and during the evening
enliven the scene by shouting and firing their six-guns into the
air. One time on the range a deer darted across Horace's path.
He shot at it but missed; suddenly another shot rang out, and
the deer dropped dead. That shot had been fired by an older
companion who had never displayed a gun. The man said, "Tell
the boys that you killed the deer."

One summer a boy of my own age who lived at the Sixty-
three Ranch went on an exploring trip with me. We tramped
up the gulch toward Buffalo Peak and saw the white-bleached
skull of a buffalo. South Park had once been a favorite Indian
hunting ground, and we picked up many flint arrowheads. Going
through the forest, we saw where a bear had been trapped and
where wood had been cut and hauled away to the salt works
some five or six miles distant. There was an abandoned log cabin
where the woodcutters had once lived, and on a nearby hill was
a lonely grave. All I ever heard about the person buried there
was told to me by my grandmother, who simply said, "Whiskey."
Killed in a drunken brawl, I guessed.

Dead Man's Gulch was some distance below the Sixty-three
Ranch, and we inspected the unmarked grave there. A man had
been found murdered in his bedroll, and the only explanation
anyone could give was that he had been killed by Mexicans
who skulked around and shot any available Anglo. For several
years after the great gold rush there were many such Mexican
bandits in California. The bandit "Joaquin Murietta," who finally
proved to be a fictitious character, gained wide publicity because
of a book bearing his name that was translated into Spanish and
gained wide distribution in Mexico and Chile.

The book, written by a San Francisco newspaperman,
depicted the abuse the Spanish-speaking people received at the
hands of men who rushed into the gold fields and despised all
so-called foreigners, especially "greasers." Many of the gold
seekers were not American citizens; and nobody had a legal title
to the land that yielded the gold. It was merely a part of the
unorganized territory that later became the state of California.

Many years later, while I was camping on a cattle ranch on the west side of the San Joaquin Valley of California, I listened to an eyewitness account of the escape of a bandit named Procoprio. The ranch was owned by Hugo Kreyenhagen, who had lived there many years. His family conducted the ranch business and in addition ran a general store that served the Mexicans who lived in the vicinity. One day the sheriff of Fresno County rode up to the store accompanied by a posse. He said that he believed Procoprio was present in a small village near the Kreyenhagen store and requested that Hugo accompany the posse to the bandit's supposed hiding place. Hugo refused to go, but said that he would walk up to the cluster of houses and determine whether or not Procoprio was present. He walked past the cluster of houses and watched a game of bowling at the rear of the houses. He then quietly opened a cabin door, and saw Procoprio asleep on a bed. He returned to the store and told the sheriff what he had seen.

The posse rode carelessly up the road. The sheriff dismounted, and abruptly opened the cabin door. Procoprio sprang from his bed and shot the sheriff dead in the doorway. Then he scooped up the sheriff's gun, fired a volley of shots, mounted one of the horses and rode away into a thicket of brush shooting and cursing the "gringos."

Although Joaquin Murietta finally proved to be fictional, I once saw in a San Francisco "museum" a human head preserved in alcohol that was labeled as his. A bounty of fifty dollars had been paid by the law-enforcing officers of the state. One editor commented that officers had at least delivered the head of a Mexican.

CHAPTER II

The Three R's

THE SALT WORKS, a good example of some early ventures, was built on a salty marsh, and it is called Bayou Salada in some records of Lieutenant Pike's exploration. Many large iron kettles were arranged over the furnaces, which used wood for fuel and a tall, well-constructed chimney to let the smoke escape. The structure still stands. My grandmother once used the salt in making butter and found it worthless because it contained many minerals besides table salt. The people who invested money to build the plant should first have evaporated some of the brine to determine its value.

When I was old enough to enter school, my folks moved to Buena Vista, about twenty miles south of my grandfather's ranch, on the western side of the Arkansas River. The wagon road passed the salt works and climbed the divide separating the drainage into the Platte River from that into the Arkansas, the divide being the boundary between the Louisiana Purchase and the land that was ceded to Mexico.

The left-hand side of Trout Creek Cañon sloped rather gently and was cut by many narrow and shallow gulches. The right-hand side of the cañon was steep and rugged. A man traveling on foot usually follows the easiest and most direct route, and doubtless the left-hand side of the cañon was first used by Indians who made narrow trails that would have been followed by Lieutenant Pike. Later, when wagons traveled through the cañon, they followed the rough Indian trails that wound uphill and downhill. When the narrow-gauge railroad was built, it had to avoid the steep hills and curve around the heads of gulches and over the points of low hills, making a wriggling course that crossed the wagon trails many times. People who now complain of the hazards of automobile travel over our paved highways should have experienced the danger encountered when riding in a horse-drawn buggy. The trip down through Trout Creek was always exciting and terrifying. Frequently at a turn of the road we suddenly would be confronted by an oncoming locomotive. The frightened horses would rear and plunge, threatening to overturn the buggy. Many people were killed in wagon and buggy wrecks.

The last trip I made with my mother down Trout Creek on our way to California was at night in a wobbling caboose at the rear of a freight train. My only recollection of that trip is of continuous "seasickness."

Historical records show that Lieutenant Pike once traveled down Trout Creek in the dead of winter and was short of grub. Finally he was placed under arrest by the Spanish authorities because he had no permission to enter their Mexican colony. Any inconveniences I may have experienced along that route, sometimes in freezing winter, were gala holidays in comparison to the hazards faced by that first American explorer.

The floor of the valley along the Arkansas River where Trout Creek poured into it was comparatively level and about four or five miles wide. The river had cut a channel about a hundred feet deep along the eastern side of the valley. At the base of a steep range of hills called Free Gold Hill was a covering of scrub piñon pines that supplied the neighborhood with much of its fuel. The western side of the valley was at the base of the mountains that are a part of the Continental Divide.

The town of Buena Vista, where I entered school and lived about five years, was well named. From it there was a beautiful view of mountain scenery. The most spectacular sights are the "collegiate peaks" Princeton, Harvard and Yale—the only colleges I knew of for years. During the summer bright-green groves of quaking aspen light up the otherwise drab landscape, and in the autumn they burst forth in beautiful spots of fiery yellow and red. During the winter the mountains are almost completely covered with snow.

We went to Buena Vista because there was a temporary
period of prosperity caused by the construction of a broad-gauge
railroad, the Colorado Midland. The road was an excellent
example of engineering, but it was built with about as little lack
of foresight as the salt works. It began nowhere and ended nowhere. It fit into no useful place in transcontinental transportation and was abandoned after several years of unprofitable
operation. It followed the general course of Trout Creek on the
right-hand side, far above the bottom of the cañon, and passed
Buena Vista at a distance of several miles, on the opposite side
of the Arkansas River.

Buena Vista was at an elevation slightly less than Fairplay.
Two narrow-gauge-railroad depots were in the town—the Denver
and South Park, and the Denver and Rio Grande. Main Street
ran straight across nearly level ground that surrounded the town.
Near the lower end of the street was a substantially built brick
courthouse and a firehouse with a bell and cupola. There were
two or three general-merchandise stores, four churches and only
two or three saloons. It was a peaceful community. One hotel
was in operation, and another stood vacant near the D. & R. G.
depot, which was abandoned as a terminal when track had been
completed up the river to flourishing Leadville.

The system of giving fire alarms centered on the fire station,
but the station was so far removed from most parts of town that
the first alarm often was the firing of six revolver shots. Such
firing was also occasionally used to attract attention to any place
where help was urgently needed. A woman who lived two doors
from the Methodist church once fired into the air to summon
help because her husband was suffering from delirium tremens.

Our brick schoolhouse contained six rooms, only four of
which were occupied when I began attending. My schoolmates
were all well behaved, and I seldom saw a fist fight. We certainly
were entitled to better treatment than was administered by one
of our teachers who had the nickname of Old Slaughterhouse.
She instilled in me the feeling that all schoolteachers were my
mortal enemies. At any slight infringement of the rules she
would summon the transgressor to her desk, make him hold out

his hand palm up and deliver five or ten sharp smacks on it with a wooden ruler. However, she did have one method of punishment which was less painful in some respects but very tedious—once I had to write the multiplication tables one hundred times on my slate because of some violation of rules. In later life I found that sort of punishment most beneficial. Fortunately, she was a rare exception to the behavior of most teachers, and she was much less severe than one I encountered later in California. I shall never forget one teacher for her kindly understanding of youngsters. Her name was Margaret Quinn. Sadly, she died giving birth to her first child. She undoubtedly would have made an excellent mother. Her funeral service was conducted in the Catholic church situated two doors from the school. I could not summon the courage to attend, but my mother, who was a devout Congregationalist of the fundamentalist type, did attend, and she reported, "I felt like a cat in a strange garret." But Mother had not a trace of bigotry in her and never criticized or ridiculed any other religion—Protestant, Catholic, Jew or whatever.

No distinction existed among my schoolmates based on wealth, because there were no really wealthy people in town. The boy in my class who lived in a slightly better house and was clothed more neatly than I was the son of a railroad station agent who drew a regular salary. For several years it was my ambition to have a similar job for myself.

Most of the houses in Buena Vista were of wooden construction. Many were infested with bedbugs that came from the forest in firewood or freshly cut lumber. Often, on waking up in the morning, I would see several bugs in the candle wax where my mother had dropped them after picking them off me while I slept.

The roaring of wind disturbs some people, but for me it arouses a homesick longing, because in the old days I often fell asleep with gales of wind lashing and loose boards rattling on the sides of our house.

Some of the rooms in many of the houses had old newspapers pasted on the walls with a mixture of flour and water. Our regular bathing facilities consisted of an ordinary washtub on the floor beside the kitchen stove. One or more kettles of water were on the stove, which had a built-in reservoir at one end. This was an iron box filled with warm water. Our source of water was a well in front of the house, with a draw bucket.

All of us children were warmly clothed and well shod in winter, because we often had to wade through a foot or more of snow in freezing weather. Most of the boys at school wore clothing of unusual appearance. One was dressed like a full-fledged cowboy, with high-heeled boots, long pants, and a bandana handkerchief with a clasp carved from a blue poker chip. Another boy, from Denver, wore a neatly pressed suit that made him look citified. He wore a white collar and a gold ring with a cameo setting. An outstanding personality was a Norwegian boy who was at least four years older than any of us and seemed a grown man. He applied himself diligently to learn English and made reasonable progress except when he tried to recite poetry from memory—for instance, "God within and heart o'er head." The most devilishly mischievous prank I ever saw at school was performed by a boy who held a dynamite cap against a nail in the fence and in the other hand held a rock poised as if to smash the cap. The explosion would undoubtedly have blown his hand off.

Besides the new railroad, other developments made my father's business more brisk. A dam was built in the Arkansas River and an electric-lighting plant constructed, only eight years after the electric bulb was invented by Edison, entirely without financial assistance from any governmental body. Many years later when I visited the town, the electric plant was still in operation.

There were few active mining operations in our vicinity. There were many abandoned shacks and tunnels, and the Arkansas River was usually muddy because of placer mining upstream. The new railroad depot on the opposite side of the river was connected with the town by a wooden bridge and a dirt road and also by a telephone line, the first I had known of.

Because our sources of amusement and entertainment were

limited, every one of them left a lasting impression. The opera house may once have been an important place, but I remember seeing only one performance, by traveling black-faced minstrels. Occasionally a show would be presented by local amateurs. Once I got free admission by working all one afternoon at tearing old newspapers into tiny scraps to be used as snowflakes in the performance. A circus came one summer, and I worked hard at carrying water to the elephant, but I was too small to gain a complimentary ticket, and I did not have the nerve to crawl under the tent. All that I saw was the parade, during which the elephant cautiously tested the strength of the bridge across Cottonwood Creek by gently placing one foot on it before venturing to proceed.

There were also some gamblers along the route practicing the shell game. The most memorable entertainment was given by traveling patent-medicine men who stood on the tailgate of a wagon under a blazing torchlight. Sometimes one of them would treat us to an exhibition of ventriloquism before expounding the virtues of his astonishing remedy. The performer who particularly impressed me was the fellow who demonstrated "Romany Oil," which he said he had discovered at the court of some Oriental potentate. It was a liniment that would cure every ailment. To demonstrate it efficiently he invited the audience to climb onto the wagon and take a treatment. One volunteer was "Deaffy" Smith, who received a thorough massage around the ears and a liberal application of the oil and finally announced that he could hear much better. Sales then began in earnest at a dollar for a one-pint bottle, three bottles for two dollars. Several years later and more than a thousand miles away I saw the same medicine and learned what the liniment really was. The only petroleum products with which I had been familiar were kerosene and axle grease, but by the time I had seen my first gasoline engine I recognized by the odor that gasoline and Romany Oil were one and the same thing.

Sunday-school Christmas celebrations always promised to bring me the one orange that I would get during the year.

One of my unpleasantest memories is that of sitting most of

one day in the one-room office of the dentist while my mother
had nearly all her teeth extracted, without any anesthetic.

A considerable number of men in our town were Union
veterans, and I would occasionally be invited to a social gathering at the local post of the G. A. R., where I could eat hardtack
and listen to stories of army life that never dealt with the
brutality of combat but were told as humorous experiences. One
man told of marching through Georgia with General Sherman
and experiencing a welcome change of diet when they camped
near a field of sweet potatoes. Next morning he strapped a large
potato on top of his knapsack. After a long day of marching
and carrying that potato—no easy thing to do—they camped in
another potato field!

A great many years later in Pasadena I called on the commander of the local G. A. R. post to ask him if he would conduct
my father's funeral service. He was most sympathetic and
obliging. In the course of our conversation he asked me in which
army my father had served. The question stumped me, because
I had never heard of any other than the Union Army. My first
answer did not clear up his question, and he asked where
my father had served. I told him, and he said, "Oh, he was in
the Army of the Potomac." When he delivered the eulogy, he
said, "The departing comrade did not have the good fortune to
have served in the Western Army; nevertheless, the Army of the
Potomac did render considerable service in the preservation of
the Union."

CHAPTER III

New Horizons

FINALLY business became so dull in Colorado that my father sold his horses and wagon and went to California, leaving my mother and me at the Parmelee Ranch for several months. The subsequent journey from Colorado to California remains only an unpleasant dream. We traveled in tourist sleeping cars with hard wooden seats that permitted the placing of boards crosswise, and on these blankets were spread. I have no recollection of how Mother and I ate during the three-day journey. When we reached San Francisco Bay and I looked out through the Golden Gate, I felt that I was at last looking at the horizon where ocean and sky met.

At about that time, a young man, F. Oskar Martin, came through the Golden Gate as a sailor before the mast. He was an immigrant from Germany and became a successful engineer.

When my parents moved to the village of Sebastopol, about sixty-five miles north of San Francisco, I stepped into a new world. The one distinctive advantage was agriculture, which could provide work for anyone who was industrious. During the first summer I earned a few dollars harvesting fruit. The name of the village was no doubt chosen by the settlers, about the time of the gold rush, because of the worldwide interest in the siege of Sebastopol during the Crimean War. Similar Americanized names shortly appeared throughout northern California adjacent to the gold mines. Only seven years after the village was named, a Masonic lodge was chartered, which indicated that the community had become thoroughly established.

At the time of the gold rush San Francisco Bay was crowded

with sailing vessels from all corners of the world. Many of the ships lay idle because their crews had deserted to search for gold. The American military commanders also lost many of their men through desertion. Men by the hundreds found no gold, and some of them returned to their homes in the East, while others settled down to develop the agricultural resources of the state. Sebastopol soon produced an abundance of fruit and vegetables for sale in San Francisco, and wild game was killed in the region to supply the city with meat.

What first struck me was the dust and cobwebs everywhere, in contrast to the clean, dry air I had known in the high mountains. Then there were the varied characters of the people—some of them old-timers, many others, like our family, recently come from the East. All the streets were merely continuations of the several intersecting dusty roads. We had one full-time church, seven saloons, and a large winery directly across the road from the church.

There were, of course, many fine, respectable people who quietly went about their affairs. But quite in contrast were the drunkards. I have never seen so many sots of different types as were always in view. Some only occasionally got tight; others were periodic performers, and we knew about when to expect to see them on Main Street. One was of such fixed habits that he deserves special mention. This was old Doc Whitson. One could almost set a clock by his two daily appearances. Early in the forenoon he would walk up the street to the winery, and late in the afternoon would weave his course back down the street, always in an angry mood.

On one side of Main Street there was an open ditch, dry in summer and a gushing torrent in winter. The ditch at one place was crossed by a footbridge consisting of a single board. One winter night during a drenching rain our neighbor heard shouts, and the lady of the house said to her husband, a mild-mannered man, "Will, somebody is shouting. You better see what the trouble is." Will lighted a lantern and went out toward the noise. Near the footbridge he saw old Doc sitting up to his arms in the water. Will politely inquired, "What are you doing, Doc?" The muffled reply was, "The inquisitiveness of a small village is appalling!"

Several hundred Chinese coolies who worked in nearby orchards made their headquarters in our town. The largest Chinatown on Main Street consisted of several houses, stores and a joss house. During their celebration of New Year's, in February, Chinatown was open house to all visitors, and I saw many strange sights. The Chinese of that time wore long queues, with their heads closely shaven except at the crown. For the shaving a customer would be seated on a stool in the open courtyard and hold a bowl beneath his chin while the barber used a long, slender blade resembling a letter opener. I saw many of the coolies smoke opium. They would come to the counter of the store, pay two bits for a small dab of "yen shee," a dark, pasty substance of about the consistency of butter, and go to a long bench covered with matting. At the head of the bench was a small shelf that served as a pillow. The addict would hold the opium on a wire, warm it over a lamp until it could be spread over the flat part of the pipe, place the pipe upside down on the lamp, inhale one long draft of the smoke, put the pipe aside and pass out completely.

A favorite drinking game was engaged in by two players. They would count in Chinese, "Yit, nee, sam, see," and so on, while holding up fingers to indicate the number. The first one who missed either the word or the signal was the loser and had to drink from a small bowl, probably some sort of wine.

I never but once saw a drunken Chinese, and that was many years later, at a sawmill high in the mountains. Early in the day I entered the dining room on a tour of inspection and saw the cook hunched over the table, dead drunk. His young coolie helper simply looked at me, with a gesture of resignation. Later on some of the mill crew found the cook in a drunken stupor on the floor of the blacksmith shop. They nailed his queue to the floor and left. Finally the helper heard the cook shouting for help and pried him loose.

On the final day of the Chinese New Year's celebration a long string of firecrackers would be hoisted above the upper balcony of the joss house, and the continued roar of the exploding crackers could be heard all along Main Street. The coolies would then leave for the orchards in single file, chattering continuously.

Most of the coolies had been imported from China to provide labor for building the Central Pacific Railroad across the Sierra Nevadas and into Nevada. They seldom brought their women with them, and they were scattered about the country working for such low wages that a white man who had a family to raise could not compete with them. They finally were excluded from our country by law. The money they earned was largely sent to relatives in China or saved to provide a fund to send their bones back to the homeland. I have seen Chinese cemeteries in the gold-mining towns of California that were merely rough heaps of earth and shallow depressions where the bodies had remained buried until the bones were finally excavated and shipped away.

One day while playing on Main Street with other boys, I saw for the first time in my life a Japanese man, walking along with a staff over his shoulder from which hung a pack. He was quite different from the coolies. He sat down on the edge of the board sidewalk and began amusing us by twisting thin rice paper into strings of flowers. Most of the boys were used to teasing the Chinese and thought to do the same with the newcomer. But he was not servile like the Chinese and quickly put us in our place.

We had three physicians of various medical schools in our village—allopathic, homeopathic and eclectic. Once I saw a doctor inspect a man lying in a wagon bound for the county hospital. One of the man's hands was tightly bandaged and greatly swollen, and he was unconscious because of the whiskey that had been administered as medicine. He had reached over a log and felt a sharp pain in his hand, and a rattlesnake had slithered away. Examination at the hospital disclosed that he had not been bitten by a snake but merely had a large redwood sliver imbedded in his hand.

Three general stores sold everything from food to clothing. The stores were open all day and during the evenings until all customers had left. Meanwhile a few men sat around the stove and the cracker barrel and exchanged news and gossip. At one such gathering a big, husky Boer boasted that he had once served in the British Army. A wizened little Irishman twitted him for having been a turncoat, and the big fellow retorted by sneering at the little fellow's religion. The meeting came to an abrupt end.

One very pleasant memory of Main Street was the care the Masonic Lodge gave to one of their members who was almost immobilized by paralysis. He was provided with a room facing out on the street from which he could wobble his rocking chair out onto the sidewalk. There people could break his loneliness by chatting with him. His meals were delivered regularly from the nearby hotel; and every forenoon when the San Francisco newspapers arrived, an elderly man with a high-pitched, monotonous voice that could be heard across the street would read him the news. The reader was a fancier of horseflesh and would often drive his high-wheeled sulky along the street at a brisk trot, flapping the reins and urging the horse along by exclaiming, "Yup, yup!" Upon the death of the lodge member, he willed a fine plot of land to the lodge, upon which they erected their permanent temple.

We had more theatrical entertainment than had been offered in Buena Vista. A troupe that accompanied a horse-drawn merry-go-round spent one winter month with us. They were all ham actors, but their performances in the town hall at least served to relieve the tedium during the season when no work could be obtained in harvesting fruit.

Fourth of July was always a noisy celebration, capped by roaring explosions of black powder put into the opening of an upturned blacksmith's anvil upon which another upturned anvil was placed. The powder then was ignited by the blacksmith's drawing a long red-hot iron across the trail of powder.

Political parades occasionally enlivened the community. Men and boys went down the street carrying torches, signs and political slogans. At that time I heard the *only* political slogan that ever had a real meaning for me: "Four more years of the full dinner pail." It was a direct appeal to the laboring man. The slogan of the other party was "Free and unlimited coinage of silver." It had no appeal to a hungry man.

The dwellings in the village were all of wood and provided with the fixtures I was already familiar with—kerosene lamps, wood-burning stoves, sometimes an open fireplace. One house we lived in was provided with a full-sized bathtub lined with zinc sheeting. It had no pipes and faucets, and hot water had to be carried to the tub from kettles on the kitchen stove.

Our schoolhouse was a well-constructed, attractive wooden building surrounded by ample playgrounds. Three rooms accommodated all eight grades. The seventh and eighth grades were in the same room, where I sat beside another boy at a shared desk. The front rows of seats were smaller than those in the rear, which were occupied by boys who were almost grown men. All the boys, with few exceptions, were well-behaved. The school district presented the only Spanish name in the entire neighborhood—Laguna School District, named after a nearby clear lake. It was entirely surrounded by trees. Those of us who went swimming in the lake always referred to it as the Lagoon. The lake had no gently sloping beaches, and in learning how to swim we went to another place, where there was a shallow muddy pool. We had no instructors and merely wallowed and flopped around until we could manage to keep afloat.

It was reported that the year before I entered that school, there had been some problems of discipline, and the trustees had hired a principal who could thrash any boy in the school. The man they chose apparently intended to satisfy his employers: he flogged every boy in his classes. A thoroughgoing martinet, he once summoned my seatmate and me, who had been whispering, to stoop over his desk and receive five strokes from a heavy mahogany cane. My black and blue marks were concealed by the seat of my trousers, and of course I did not report the incident to my parents. The mahogany cane was finally broken while being used on a defiant boy named Dino, whose people owned the vineyard and winery opposite the church. He refused to come forward, and the principal stepped to the rear of the room, dragged him forward by the collar, turned him over the desk and gave him such a severe flogging that the cane broke.

One favorable recollection I have of that harsh principal was his showing us a medallion about the size of a half-dollar. He passed it around and told us that the new metal of which it was made was aluminum.

We lived one year in a house directly across the road from the church. Revival meetings began on New Year's Eve and continued for a month or more. I attended one meeting and then discovered that I could hear the services well enough without leaving home. There were loud songs and passionate pleadings with sinners to repent and escape eternity in fire and damnation, interrupted by shouts of "Amen, brother!" and "Glory hallelujah!"

After graduating from the eighth grade I got a job as errand boy at the drugstore, with a regular monthly wage of six dollars, which for an entire year would about equal two or three months in the orchard. I managed to spend some time, too, in such places as the pool hall. That tour of employment in the drugstore turned out favorably for me, because there I met a young man who had become a licensed pharmacist. He was neatly dressed, with his forelock long enough to fall over his eyes, a style fashionable among some young men. He recounted his thrilling experiences as a high-school student and dwelt at length on events on the "campus," which, I later found out, was merely a small part of a city block. He inspired me with ambition to continue my schooling at Santa Rosa, some six or seven miles distant and reached by passenger train. The fare plus the monthly attendance fee for students from outside the district amounted to some six dollars a month, which I had to earn during the summer vacations.

Entering high school was one of the most inspiring and exhilarating experiences of my life. The teachers were all well educated and dedicated to improving the minds of their pupils. Discipline was maintained with no mention of physical punishment. Many entirely new subjects were presented to me—history, English, literature, French, Latin, biology, physics, chemistry, geometry, algebra. Only a few other Sebastopol boys attended high school. Two of my friends had to drop out before completing the three-year course to care for their aging parents, being the youngest in their families.

A teacher with whom I became thoroughly acquainted was Charles D. Snyder, who had recently graduated from Stanford, which he had worked his way through by waiting on tables. His specialty was biology, and he ultimately became a member of the faculty of Johns Hopkins University. At our high school he taught many other subjects, such as chemistry, physics and geometry, all of which I studied.

At the end of each school day I had to wait two hours for the train home. During that time I often sat in the railroad car and solved problems in geometry for pure pleasure. We had no textbooks, merely mimeographed papers stating the theorems.

Some people are unable to grasp and appreciate geometry, while others may not appreciate poetry or music. I have successfully coached youngsters who were struggling with geometry. My last effort at coaching was a complete failure, and I turned to the latest textbook to find some reason for it. It gave no new information. Apparently it had been written to provide teachers with problems by which they might convince pupils that geometry could have some *practical* use. Geometry certainly serves practical purposes, especially in some branches of engineering; but its primary value is that of training in logical thinking, and the old proverb "There is no royal road to geometry" is still valid.

The public library in Santa Rosa was very good, and I spent many hours there after school. Once I picked up a classic publication of the United States Geological Survey that gave a full description of ore deposits at Leadville and much other information. Shortly after that I asked my favorite teacher, Charlie

Synder, for advice about my becoming a mining engineer. He said that one of his college mates had done quite well in that profession and urged me to go to Stanford. Many years later he revealed to me that his successful college friend was Herbert Hoover, who roomed with him at Encina Hall. Hoover graduated a year earlier than Snyder and returned to visit him shortly before the next commencement. He asked what plans Snyder had to celebrate that week, said, "You'll probably need some money," and then laid a twenty-dollar gold coin on the desk.

During my high-school days I heard my first political speech. It was given by Thomas B. Reed, Speaker of the House of Representatives. Since it was strictly a partisan affair, the faculty could not, of course, grant permission for the students to be absent from school, and even intimated that absentees might be disciplined. The meeting was held in the large hall near the race track, and a majority of the students were present. I remember very little of what Reed said, except, "The Republican party successfully conducted the Civil War." A candidate for Congress who also spoke lamented the unseemliness of some women who were lowering and degrading their sex by wanting to vote and enter politics.

High-school graduation ceremonies took place in a large public theater. I was chosen to introduce the students who were to deliver essays. That task was simple, but when it came to introducing the principal invited guest, a university professor, I was out of my element. I tried to pronounce a word unknown to me—*pedagogy*. A titter swept the audience at my attempt. In our graduating class there were thirty students, and only four or five went on to college. At that time Stanford and the University of California at Berkeley were the outstanding colleges on the Pacific Coast.

The American people are both generous and sentimental and are apt to be swept off their feet by an emotional tidal wave when some humanitarian cause presents itself. Such a burst of emotion occurred during my final year in high school when the slogans "Remember the Maine!" "Hurrah for Cuba!" "To hell with Spain!" flashed across the country. The source of our enthusiasm was yellow-journal accounts of the horrible abuse of the Cuban people by the Spanish government; and the Spanish-American War began. It was short. We freed the Cuban people from the rule of Spain and then left them to govern themselves, a task for which they were not prepared. Now they are under Communist dictatorship.

CHAPTER IV

College Life and Stanford Farm

AFTER GRADUATING from high school, I went to work in the orchard and hop field near my home. Late in autumn I had accumulated enough money to enter Stanford as a "Christmas freshman." My supply of cash was far below what was recommended by the university, but I was determined to at least get my foot inside the door, even though most of the courses I wanted to study had begun in the fall semester, and only one, physics, was of real use. But—I *had arrived!*

Stanford University had an enrollment of only 1,087 students, of whom 729 lived in California, 333 came from thirty-six other states, and 25 students came from seven foreign countries. The faculty consisted of 43 professors, 18 associate professors and 19 assistant professors. The total faculty members averaged about twelve students for each instructor, and we were able to get into close contact with the educators.

The first few days after I enrolled I stayed with a former high-school classmate. He was supporting himself in his own shop, where he repaired shoes. He was living in The Camp, a frame building formerly occupied by workmen who had erected the stone buildings on the campus. It consisted of about a dozen comfortable rooms renting for three dollars a month. There was a nearby restaurant run by a Chinese where a substantial meal cost fifteen cents.

I saw a Negro for the first time—a handsome young man enrolled as a student.

There was no charge for tuition, aside from the registration fee of ten dollars for each of the two semesters. But even with the low cost of living, I possessed only enough cash to last

scarcely more than one month. Soon, however, I got a job waiting
on table in a private boardinghouse in Palo Alto, so I earned
my food and enough money to room with another old high-school
pal, in a building owned by Major Norris, a veteran of the
Civil War.

About that time the United States began sending troops to
Manila, and a company of militia in San Francisco recruited
men on the Stanford campus.

About eighty students enrolled. They served in the Philip-
pines for about a year, and then most of them resumed their
college courses. Two lost their lives in combat.

One of the boys, John M. Switzer, after his discharge remained in Manila, where he prospered in business. Some twenty
years later I met him in San Francisco at a luncheon, and he
related some of his experiences. In his explorations he had noted
the poorly marked grave of Ferdinand Magellan, the celebrated
navigator, who died in the Philippine Islands, April 27, 1521.
Switzer brought the matter to the attention of other Americans,
and they decided to improve the grave site. An iron fence was
suggested, and part of such a structure was finally located in
the basement of a church. Upon their inquiry of the parish priest,
he asked why they wanted to buy the fence and upon hearing
of their purpose informed them that it had long ago been
brought from Spain for that same purpose. They found that only
three sides had ever arrived, and they had to construct the
fourth side.

There had been wide rumors that the Japanese might invade
the islands, and when someone asked for Switzer's opinion, he
replied, "Certainly the Japanese can invade the islands, but
they can't hold them."

Many of the Stanford boys were eager to enlist, and I wrote
to my father for advice. He replied that he did not think the
country was in great need of men in the service, so I dismissed
the matter from my mind. Some of the boys who were physically
unfit for military service were still eager to become soldiers and
regularly visited Major Norris to seek advice. One young
fellow who wore thick glasses discarded them and memorized

the letters on the chart used by examining doctors. One day my roommate asked the major if he thought we might enter the army. His reply was, "You're damned right. If a couple of raw country boys like you want to keep out of the army, you'd better stay away from the recruiting sergeant."

During the following summer I earned enough money to nearly pay the room rent of five dollars a month in the men's dormitory, Encina Hall, and I paid for my board by waiting on table at various houses on the campus.

Encina Hall was a four-story stone building. It was the first house I had lived in that had modern facilities, including hot and cold running water and electric lighting. The electricity was steam-generated by a powerhouse on the campus that used coal for fuel. The power stopped at ten-thirty sharp, and we were given warning a half hour earlier by a slight dimming of the lights. We then had to depend on candles. Kerosene lamps were prohibited because of the fire hazard.

During my final semester I was elected president of Encina Club. The only noteworthy event during my term of office occurred at our final stag party, held in a spacious clubroom that originally had been the dining hall. An odd character had wandered onto the campus, at least sixty years ahead of his time. His wavy hair reached down to his shoulders. He wore a black derby hat and a togalike garment extending to his knees, below which were knee stockings and low black shoes. He became known as The Blanket Man and attracted attention as he strolled about the quadrangle. Quickly surrounded, between classes, by curious crowds, he would produce a Bible from within his toga, read a few verses, make a short religious speech and move on. He often was entertained at the fraternity houses, and finally he came to our stag party as an uninvited guest. Apparently he made some uncomplimentary remarks about college men in general; and when I saw an unofficial committee escorting him out the door, protocol seemed to demand that I should follow. They went down the steps along a paved walk and seemed about to discontinue their march when suddenly a tall, gangling hurdler sprang onto the back of our departing guest

and encircled him with a grasp like a boa constrictor. A hunky
football player stepped forward and out of thin air produced a
pair of horse clippers and proceeded to mow the long hair down
to the scalp, leaving only one long lock hanging behind the
left ear. The fellow was then released. The road to Palo Alto
was pointed out to him, and he was told to follow it and not
return.

This performance was a prize story to newsmen and was
written up in many papers. In one such town The Blanket Man
spoke before a religious group and described the barbaric
treatment he had received at our hands.

The following week my major professor, Dr. J. C. Branner,
and his wife graciously entertained at dinner all of us who were
about to graduate. There were about a dozen guests seated at
the table, and the story of The Blanket Man became a principal
topic of conversation. The only guest who lived in Encina, I
maintained a discreet silence and was greatly relieved when
Branner, who was acting president of the university, finally said,
"I have received a lot of information which you did not get and
you are not going to get. That man was pure faker."

Encina Hall housed about two hundred boys, many of whom
were as short of cash as myself, while others were comparatively
rich. There was no discrimination on the basis of religion. There
were many Jewish boys among us. Those who came from small
towns had apparently never been discriminated against and
naturally fitted into our group quite unnoticed. The Jewish boys
who came from San Francisco were slightly reserved and clan-
nish because they had been discriminated against in "The City";
however, they quickly responded to our friendly feeling and became ordinary members of our group.

Encina Hall students followed, among them, all the different
courses offered by the university, and we all gained a wide range
of knowledge beyond our individual specialties. Many years later
I walked past the Hall with my favorite professor, "J. P." Smith,
who was respected and loved by all his students. I remarked
that I had obtained more education in the dormitory than in the
classrooms. He said, "I haven't the slightest doubt of that. I

always told the boys they could learn more from each other than we could teach them." The Hall is no longer used as a dormitory. It has been rebuilt and strengthened by steel reinforcement.

The Hall had become terribly overcrowded when recently I visited a young man there. With three or four boys in one room, it resembled an old cowpunchers' bunkhouse. Fortunately the outer appearance of the building had not changed. As I walked through vacant rooms that had not yet been repaired, I could almost hear the plaintive refrain of "Empty Saddles in the Old Corral."

Looking back on the four years I was privileged to live on what had once been the privately owned Stanford Farm, the most pleasant memory I have is of walking with my mother along a roadside path, near the arboretum. Mrs. Stanford drove past in her elegant carriage, scarcely an arm's length away from us. She bowed, and smiled as graciously as if we were long-time friends.

Another time a group of students called at her campus residence to welcome her back after an extended absence. As we stood on the lawn she came out on the porch and thanked us, saying, "I am very glad to be back again with *my boys.*"

Mrs. Stanford was a devoutly religious woman and was interested in the work of the early Spanish padres who established the missions. She was one of the first contributors to the restoration of San Carlos Mission, near Carmel, which was in ruinous condition. The chapel was littered with rubble, and the greatest concern of the priest who was in charge of reconstruction was that the grave of Junipero Serra, in front of the altar, should not be disturbed. Final removal of the rubble in front of the altar and careful examination proved that nothing had been damaged; yet all nearby Spanish missions had been desecrated.

The baptismal font was missing, and it was finally located in the adjoining countryside, where it had been used as a watering trough for cattle.

Fortunately Mrs. Stanford was spared the anguish of seeing

destruction of the beautiful chapel erected in memory of her husband. She died February 28, 1905. The great earthquake occurred more than a year later, April 18, 1906.

Will Irwin has written a good account of early days on the Stanford campus.[1]

The boys who lived in Encina behaved themselves. Only a handful, some of them geniuses, used hard liquor, and most of these were expelled for various reasons, such as petty theft. Occasionally a few of us would walk to the neighboring village at Mayfield, Palo Alto being bone dry, and we would sit at a large round table in the barroom of an old-fashioned country hotel. We drank beer and carved our initials on the table. Several similarly decorated tabletops were displayed on the walls, and finally the number grew so large that they were all removed and displayed at an "establishment" in Menlo Park. Many years later my son, who was attending college there, escorted me to a table that he had discovered after many hours of searching. He pointed out my initials; they had been carved very small, demonstrating that I had cut no great figure in student affairs, even in drinking circles.

We were policed by four or five of our companions selected by the faculty's Student Affairs Committee, the court of last decision on questions involving misconduct. The annual register stated the rules of conduct: "In the government of the University the largest liberty consistent with good work and good order is allowed. Students are expected to show within and without the University such respect for order, morality, personal honor, and the rights of others as demanded of good citizens. Failure to do this will be sufficient cause for removal from the University."

Politics involving elections of officers for the student body was one of our outstanding extracurricular activities at Encina Hall, though only a few Encina men chose politics for their life's work. Among those few was Senator Carl T. Hayden of Arizona, who has continuously held public office after graduation. He had a very pleasing personality, and newspapermen have rated him

---

[1] William H. Irwin, *The Making of a Reporter,* 1942.

one of the most influential members of the Senate, because of the many kindnesses shown by him to his fellow members. The Senator has good-humoredly remarked that the only election he ever lost was in 1898, when he ran for the office of president of the student body of Stanford.

Another of my companions at Encina who made an enviable record as a public servant was John (Jack) T. Nourse, Jr., who was elected Judge of the Superior Court in San Francisco, later appointed a member of the Appellate Court, and thereafter elected and continuously re-elected as Presiding Justice. He served for many years as a trustee of the university.

Chester Naramore, who was one of the Encina "police force," served with the United States Geological Survey for several years and later on, at the beginning of World War I, became chief of the Petroleum Department of the Bureau of Mines. He was sent to Europe to report on how petroleum products from America were being divided and used by our own forces and those of our allies. He sailed on a troopship that was under the British flag and was there greeted by his friend, Herbert Hoover, who asked why he was not in uniform and then was quite surprised to learn that he was in the diplomatic service.

The record shows that Naramore was a shirt-sleeve diplomat who used direct language. One day during the voyage he saw a G.I. knock a member of the ship's crew down a stairway for an insulting remark. Hoover wanted the affair reported to the American commander, but Naramore promptly protested. "No, Chief," he said. "That limey got what was coming to him." At the conclusion of the war he became an executive for a large oil company and directed geological surveys in North Africa.

Oswald S. Lowsley was an intimate friend of mine at Encina. He finished his medical education at Johns Hopkins and gained an international reputation for research and practice in urology. Some of his patients were men of great prominence. On my last visit with him he said, "Nobody can say that any person ever failed to receive my care because he had no money." He then related an experience that he compared to a tale from the *Arabian Nights*. A wealthy man from a foreign country arranged for treatment at a New York hospital. With his request for admittance he attached many unusual requests, such as rooms for several of his assistants. After some inconvenience Lowsley arranged for the necessary space. The man failed to appear at the appointed time, and Lowsley called off the deal. A few days later the secretary of the wealthy man visited Lowsley and begged that his employer be treated. He received instructions from Lowsley that the Mr. Big should report at an exact hour on a certain date. The treatment was successful, and Lowsley inquired at an important bank as to his patient's financial worth, and it was indicated that the man certainly had in excess of one hundred million dollars—possibly five times that. Lowsley billed him for one hundred thousand dollars, which was protested, and the fee was reduced to not less than fifty thousand dollars, I believe, which was promptly paid.

During one of his frequent lecturing tours in Europe, Dr. Lowsley visited the native city of his former wealthy patient. He was lavishly entertained and was presented with expensive gifts, one of which was a beautiful water color painting. Lowsley refused this gift because of the high export tax he would have to pay and chose instead a cheaper oil painting. When he arrived at the port of exit, he was confronted by a customs official who demanded evidence of his identity. Lowsley produced his badge as an honorary member of the New York police force. The official exclaimed, "Oh, I know all about you. Your picture has appeared in many of our newspapers." He then asked what items Lowsley wished to export. Lowsley pointed to a large collection, and the official directed that the entire lot should be passed without any inspection.

Andrew J. Copp, Jr., was an intimate friend of mine and Lowsley's at Encina. For many years he conducted a successful law practice at Los Angeles, and during World War II he served as a member of the Judge Advocate General's staff, retiring with the rank of colonel.

George Cromwell followed his profession of civil engineer and became a recognized authority in hydraulic engineering in

San Diego County, where he recently was buried with full military honors for his service in World War I.

Nearly half the students at Stanford lived on campus—194 men in fraternity houses, 82 women in sorority houses, about 100 women in Roble Hall dormitory and about 200 in Encina Hall. The remainder lived in Palo Alto and other towns as far distant as twenty miles.

In student political affairs there was a sharp division between fraternity men and the "barbarians" who usually dominated at election time. Such a division did not, of course, prevail in later years.

Among the foreign students living at Encina was Charles Eliseo Cortes, from Guadalajara, Mexico. He graduated as a civil engineer; and on returning to his home city, he successfully practiced his profession with the special distinction accorded his title of engineer. He later became mayor of the city and remained so until the outbreak of the revolution that ended the thirty-year dictatorship of Porfirio Díaz. When Cortes received a telegram ordering him to report at Mexico City, he correctly interpreted the order and immediately boarded a train for California. The last time I talked with him he said he hoped that an American army would enter Mexico. When I said that that was not probable, he shrugged in Mexican fashion. He was later employed by a large oil company operating in California and foreign countries.

Another Encina boy from Mexico City was Valentine Richard Garfias, whose father had been postmaster general during the Díaz regime. Valentine had once been a cadet in the national military academy. He came to California to learn English, which would assist him in business in Mexico. He graduated from a private preparatory school, and some of the faculty persuaded him to enter Stanford. He first registered in the civil engineering department, headed by Professor Charles D. Marx, familiarly known as "Daddy" Marx because of the personal interest he took in all of his students, particularly freshmen. "Garf" later told me of his first interview with Professor Marx. He was asked if he had studied French. When Garf said yes, he was advised to enter a class in that language, because it would help him in perfecting his English. How he became more proficient in English as the years passed is illustrated by a story he told me of his first attempt to translate a French story into English. "I stood up and began to read a description of a beautiful girl. She was a peach. I came to one word which I could not remember. The correct translation for it was either *dimple* or *pimple*. I just took a stab and said 'pimple.' The whole class roared, and I just grabbed my book and beat it out of the room."

Another story about Garf came from my classmate Dave Folsom, who was present at a congressional hearing in Washington involving some Mexican-versus-American interests in oil. I repeated the story at my last meeting with Garfias and his wife, when they were entertaining my daughter and me at lunch. Evidently Maria had never heard the story, and later she expressed her appreciation. Dave's story was: "The American interests employed a very eloquent lawyer to present their case. Garf could speak English as well as any person in the room, but when he arose to speak, he put on his Mexican accent, and said, 'Gentlemen, we are just poor people; we cannot afford to hire expensive lawyers.' His speech knocked the lawyer's effort into a cocked hat."

At the outbreak of the Mexican revolution Garfias realized that with his background it would be suicidal to return to his native land. Many refugees fled to California, and at a meeting Garfias cautioned some of the most belligerent, "Let's not make fools of ourselves. Remember, we are simply guests in this country." He remained many years in the United States but never relinquished his Mexican citizenship. After a successful career as a director of one of America's largest oil companies, he finally retired to Mexico, where he became a trustee of the National University of Mexico.

With the outbreak of the Mexican revolution, there was naturally violent anti-American feeling, for Díaz had given more consideration to foreign capitalists than to his own poverty-stricken people. "From 1913 to 1915 more than seventy Americans were slain in Mexico. By 1913 there were over fifty thousand Americans in Mexico, and their investments totaled about a billion dollars, more than those of all other foreign nations combined. The State Department repeatedly warned Americans to leave." [2]

Many American mining engineers told me of the hardships they endured in escaping from Mexico. An account of an astonishing experience was told to me by an old-time friend, Hunt, in the California oil fields. He and a number of other Americans started to leave Mexico but were stopped at Tampico by howling mobs that surrounded their hotel. Two warships lay in the harbor. One was German and the other British, both within hearing distance of the mob. In the forenoon the German commander called on the British commander and inquired what he proposed to do. The Englishman replied that his country was at peace with Mexico and he could therefore do nothing. In the afternoon the German officer again called on the British commander and received the same answer. The German then said that there were women and children besieged by the mob and he intended to land marines to escort them to a ship lying at the wharf. He carried out his purpose, and my friend told me, "So help me God, if it had not been for those German marines, my bones would now lie bleaching in Mexico."

After my friend and some other Americans reached the United States, they visited our Secretary of the Navy, Josephus Daniels. The Secretary was entirely ignorant of the geography of the Gulf of Mexico, and turning to a map to find where Tampico was, began to trace his finger along the shore line beginning at the side of the gulf exactly at the opposite side, in the peninsula of Yucatán.

A few years later we were at war with Germany. The California legislature passed a law forbidding the teaching of German in our public schools. *Hamburger* steak was changed to *Liberty* steak, and the Haus of Brau changed its name to American Restaurant.

---

[2] Thomas A. Bailey, *The American Pageant*, 1956.

An opportunity was once presented to students from Stanford and the University of California to participate in an effort to ensure an honest election in San Francisco. An organization of reputable citizens contributed money and directed the movement. We were furnished free transportation to and from San Francisco and were paid five dollars to stand at the polling places during the night to observe and record the counting of ballots. "Corporals" chosen from among our group patrolled several polling places to see how things were progressing. I never heard that there was any trouble, in contrast with some elections, when a voter might get his block knocked off if he fought the dictates of some political boss.

Some of the hardest labor I ever performed was as a stevedore on the waterfront at Vallejo, the town where my parents lived. Freshly cut and water-soaked redwood lumber was shoved over the rail of a ship onto the wharf, and we carried it away and piled it up. An even tougher job was that at Mare Island navy yard, where a dry dock was being constructed. We had to move gravel, sand and cement in wheelbarrows, then mix and turn the material with shovels. I felt well paid when I sometimes earned slightly more than two dollars a day.

CHAPTER V

Gold-mining Experience

IMMEDIATELY after I was graduated from Stanford, in 1902, I was fortunate to get a job as draftsman with the State Mining Bureau, thanks to the good offices of a college friend who was temporarily employed there. The large drafting-room window in the Ferry Building afforded a front-row-center view of the City Beside the Golden Gate, which I have since felt to be my old home town, directly up Market Street to Twin Peaks. Most of the buildings on both sides of the street were destroyed by the earthquake and fire of 1906.

One of my Encina friends, Joe Hamilton, greatly improved his reputation as an advertising man by painting a huge sign on a steel girder of a department store: "We shall rebuild as soon as the bricks cool," which reflected the spirit of San Franciscans after the disaster. The Ferry Building, erected by the state, was not badly damaged, nor were most of the buildings erected by the federal government, such as the mint, the customhouse and the post office. In contrast the city hall was a total wreck, reflecting poor workmanship and a graft-ridden city administration.

The skyline seen from my window showed two high advertisements. On the left was a picture of the globe and a bucket of paint dripping down and nearly covering the globe. On the right was a large sign "Ice Cold Steam 5¢," which mystified eastern tourists arriving on the ferries from the Oakland shore of San Francisco Bay.

The odor of freshly roasted coffee often came through the open window. By recent figures coffee is the most important import coming through the Golden Gate.

At noon there was always a large crowd of laboring men, such as stevedores, in front of the Ferry Building, and once I witnessed an exhibition of showmanship far exceeding that of the peddler of Romany Oil. The performer was a dentist displaying his skill in extracting teeth painlessly. His stage setting, on a horse-drawn dray, was inspiring and consisted of a fully equipped dental office. After a spiel that attracted a crowd he invited someone to come up and have a tooth pulled. A hulking man climbed the steps and sat in the operating chair. After administering the anesthetic, the dentist continued his amusing chatter and finally grasped his forceps, yanked out the tooth and held it up for display. Then he turned to the patient and asked if it had been painful. The man poked his finger into the cavity and replied, "It didn't hurt a goddam bit!" The dentist turned to his audience, saying, "We seldom recommend that the patient insert an unsterilized finger in the open wound."

In the early forenoon during the racing season at a track across the bay the streetcars would be loaded with passengers, many of whom were obviously gamblers, bartenders and the like, accompanied by their lady friends.

The State Mining Bureau had been established many years before. It had from time to time been headed by men who were well qualified to conduct scientific and technical investigations, and some excellent reports were published. However, many men had been occasionally employed whose reports were not worth the paper they were printed on. The official head of the bureau was the State Mineralogist; that officer at the time of my employment was devoid of any training in scientific matters, and the bureau had become encrusted with political barnacles. The one exception was E. B. Preston, about seventy years of age and a graduate of the mining school at Freiburg, Germany. His sole duty was to make simple tests of mineral samples that had been mailed in for identification.

An outstanding employee was Charles G. Yale, who was also employed by the Geological Survey. Part of his time was spent at the Ferry Building and the remainder at the United States Mint. His principal occupation was to compile statistics on the current production of gold, which was difficult because many gold producers were secretive, not wishing to reveal their income. Yale had been a newspaperman almost from the earliest days of gold mining and had established a personal relationship with many of the most influential mining men, who trusted him. His reputation was so high that the Geological Survey obtained a special dispensation that resulted in his services being retained after he had reached sixty-five.

I was very fortunate to gain an intimate friendship with Yale, and it was of great benefit to me. His father, Gregory Yale, was a lawyer who came to California shortly after the great gold rush. Charlie missed being a Native Son of the Golden West because his mother returned to Florida to give birth to her first child; but he grew up in San Francisco, swam in a pond near the site of the present Palace Hotel and hunted quail in the sand hills where Larkin Street was later developed. He witnessed a public hanging conducted by a vigilance committee.

Charlie Yale's experience in mining affairs was not confined to a desk in some newspaper office. One of his early ventures was in the booming mining camp of Julian, some distance east of San Diego. Some of the claims that had been staked by the miners were found to be within the limits of a Spanish land grant and therefore could not be legalized. The government sent a surveying crew to trace the boundary line of the grant, and many of the miners, including Yale, went out with the intention of driving the chief surveyor away. He calmly walked forward, faced the irate group, and said, "You could kill me if you wanted to, but that would do you no good because the government would send another man to locate the boundary line." The miners retreated crestfallen to their cabins.

When the gold rush into Alaska occurred, Yale went there as a newspaper correspondent, and he knew where to get a good story. A top-flight correspondent was surprised at a story of Yale's and asked how he had got it. Yale told me later, "I visited with all the boys in their cabins, where some of them were lousy." The other fellows were too dainty to enter such places.

At one time Yale was editor of the *Engineering and Mining*

Journal in New York, but he did not remain long on that assignment. "It was cold as the devil, and I had no friends in the town," he said.

The famous Bohemian Club was organized while Charlie was a young man, and he was practically a charter member. After his retirement from government service the club elected him librarian and gave him permanent living quarters in the clubhouse, where I often visited him. When he first escorted me into the library, he remarked, "A man died in here once, and it was three days before anybody found the body." One day as we were leaving the club I saw a huge bronze plaque on the wall in memory of Bret Harte, and I inquired if he had been a member of the club. Charlie's reply was, "Hell, no. Nobody liked him." Later, however, I found that the celebrated author's name was indeed on the membership roll, which merely shows that nothing succeeds like success.

An opportunity to visit the gold-mining regions in Tuolumne County was afforded me during my last two months' service with the Mining Bureau. Tuolumne County has many historical features that are worthy of passing note. It was supposed to have been the headquarters of Joaquin Murietta, the great and fictitious Mexican bandit, and the choice of that site by his author is quite appropriate because old maps show Sonoran Camp and American Camp, and a much later map shows Chinese Camp.

A famous stage robber operated somewhere in Tuolumne County. Black Barte was a very gentlemanly highwayman and sometimes wrote poetry of a sort. He was finally apprehended in San Francisco through the cuff of a shirt that bore a laundry mark, indicating his high social standing.

Another old townsite that attracted my attention was Second Garrote, where, it was said, two men were hanged at the same time from the same tree.

I covered the nearly two hundred square miles where any mining operations had been carried on. There were five producing mines in the county at the time of my visit and many dozens that had been called mines or were in process of trying to become mines, which illustrates a statement made by the famous mining engineer Herbert Hoover, that "gold mining on the average is not a profitable business and is no business for amateurs."

My education had provided me only with the fundamentals of the sciences of geology and chemistry, and of civil and mechanical engineering. I soon was convinced that I knew nothing about mining. I wanted to get underground while I was in Tuolumne County but was unable to do so. It was just as well, for I would not have learned anything from the little I saw, groping along with no light other than a tallow candle.

I saw one old prospector with his donkey and all his equipment loaded on the animal, hoping to find a mine. I stayed several nights with prospectors who were trying to develop a mine in the outlying district.

I did learn one thing, from some Cornish miners who had a shallow excavation near Tuttle Town on Jackass Hill, where Mark Twain once lived and claimed to have been a miner. They pointed out a quartz vein and described the hanging wall and foot wall and the gouge. It was the first time I had ever inspected a quartz vein that might contain gold. I observed during several years that the Cornish miners were very courteous and glad to show a neophyte mining engineer something about practical mining.

A mine named Rawhide stood idle when I visited the county. It had once been very profitable, and years later a mining company took it over to do some additional prospecting and development under the guidance of an engineer friend of mine, John C. Moulton. They unwatered the lower workings of the mine and did considerable prospecting. All they found was a human skeleton at the bottom of the shaft, which bears out another axiom of Herbert Hoover's, that "an old gold mine is never allowed to die in peace."

I saw an unusual gold-mining operation in the town of Sonora. The main street, like that of most other early mining camps, followed near the bottom of a gulch. A business building on the street had recently burned down, and the owner of the vacant lot was engaged in sluicing out gold there. He took me down to the sluice box. It was full of muddy water, and I did not see much of anything, but he stuck his thumb down into the water and picked out a gold nugget the size of a pea. His mining operations yielded enough profits to replace his old building with a new one constructed of brick.

At the old town of Columbia, which is now a state park and is worth a visit by any tourist because it has retained its original appearance, "Benny" Pownell was the Wells Fargo agent, and one of his hired men who had been cleaning out an irrigation ditch found a gold nugget the size of a small carrot and displayed high integrity by bringing it to his employer. The old Wells Fargo office contained the balances in which gold was weighed.

The largest mine in operation was the Eagle-Shawmut, in charge of an educated Cornishman named Charles Uren, whose son, Lester, attended the University of California and started one of the first courses in petroleum engineering.

It is well worth while for any tourist to view the beautiful scenery along State Highway 88 over Tioga Pass, at an elevation of 8,573 feet. The Tioga mine was located near the summit of the mountains, and much of the road leading up to the mine was originally constructed by the Tioga Mining Company, financed by men who had made their wealth in whaling. The privately owned road later came into the possession of the state of California through the efforts of the Sierra Club. Motorists fail to see the beautiful scenery because they drive so fast. The best way is on foot, as I did one season with the Sierra Club.

Several interesting geological formations will present themselves to the tourist if he enters the county on its westward boundary. Several large veins of white quartz are readily observable, part of a long series of such veins originally called the Mother Lode. Gold usually occurs in quartz, but much of the quartz veins are relatively bare of gold.

Another interesting geological sight is Table Mountain. It is capped by black igneous rock which had flowed down an old stream bed and was harder than the surrounding rock, so that erosion left Table Mountain above the average ground surface.

Several other old stream beds contained gold that was uncovered by drift mining in various localities along the western side of the Sierra Nevadas.

After I finished my tour of inspection, which was really nothing more than gathering statistics on the depths of each mine, how many men were employed and the name of the manager, my information was published, together with a map of the county showing the mines and prospects.

I decided that I must get practical experience at some place where active gold-mining operations were in progress.

CHAPTER VI

Underground Mining at Grass Valley

I WENT to Grass Valley, which is one of the oldest mining towns in California and where hard-rock mining had its inception. Grass Valley and Nevada City, only five miles apart, were first settled by Americans at the time of the great gold rush of 1849. The two towns were connected by an electric railway and were on the narrow-gauge railway that began at Colfax on the main line of the Central Pacific. I first stayed a few days at the old National Hotel in Nevada City and there read my first press notice in the local paper. It gave my name and said that I was "from San Francisco engaged in the mining business." I talked to an old-timer who had taken placer gold from Dear Creek, but he had not prospered. The amount of gold he washed out of the gravel soon became so heavy that it could not be conveniently carried about, and he merely spent his earnings.

Some of the earliest lode mines in California were started at Grass Valley, and the town saw a continuous stream of young college men who considered it a sort of graduate school of mining engineering.[1]

From Grass Valley I walked to the North Star mine, a distance of a mile or more, and presented a card of introduction to Edwin L. Oliver, a graduate of the University of California and member of a well-to-do family. He read the card and said, "Mr. Yale was a great friend of my father." He then introduced me to the superintendent of the mine, A. D. Foote, a civil engineer from Yale. Foote told me, "I don't know whether we can use you or not. We just hired a young engineer last week." I told

---

[1] John Hays Hammond, *Autobiography*, 1935; Herbert C. Hoover, *Memoirs*, 1951.

him I could run a pick and shovel or wheelbarrow, and he said, "Oh, hell! Anyone can do that. Come to work next Monday."

My first day underground was one that I shall never forget. I was carrying the rear end of the steel tape line, the front end of which was held by the young engineer who had been hired earlier, Erol MacBoyle. Oliver was handling the transit. We were engaged in making a survey up toward the bottom of the old inclined shaft, which had followed the original vein down from the surface for a distance of about 2,300 feet.

We had to scramble up over rough, broken granite rock that was soaking wet and reeking with nitroglycerine fumes. I retched every few steps, and for several days thereafter the back of my head felt as if somebody were pounding it with a hammer. Such an encounter with nitroglycerine fumes was called by miners "eating powder smoke." Apparently I was more sensitive to powder smoke than the other members of the crew. I have, however, seen men working in the open air, on the surface, merely pushing a car of ore from a chute to the mill who were overcome by the fumes from the broken ore.

Edwin Oliver later amassed a considerable fortune by inventing and manufacturing apparatus to continuously filter gold-bearing solutions out of slime that would quickly choke an ordinary filter. He was later elected president of the American Institute of Mining Engineers.

MacBoyle did very well for himself by taking over the old Idaho-Maryland mine that in earlier days had been a profitable producer but when I first saw it was standing full of water. A company of eastern capitalists unwatered the old mine, but apparently the manager, who previously had been in command of the Colorado National Guard, which was engaged in putting down riotous trouble at Cripple Creek, was an extravagant operator, and his backers let him down completely.

MacBoyle secured an option on the property, which was then free of water, and he let out leases on certain blocks of ore to miners. Under such an arrangement the company furnished the tools and powder and the lessees received a part of the net proceeds from the gold that was milled and refined.

This system of leasing out blocks of ground to miners was an old Cornish custom. The lessees were called tributers, and the block of ground assigned to each one was called the tribute pitch. Unfortunately, MacBoyle did not live many years to enjoy his good fortune.

Each month we made an underground survey of all new development work done the previous month, and we measured and mapped the areas of the stopes from which ore had been removed. MacBoyle usually handled the transit, and I handled one end of the tape. The other end of the tape was handled by a scrawny little Cornishman known as Sammy Bellwire because his usual employment was to plod up and down the stairways of the old, original shaft and make sure that the Cornish pump was in operation and that the bellwire signaled to the hoisting engineer whether or not to lower or raise the skip. Sammy was illiterate, but he had an excellent memory. He never took notes, and when we were making the final survey at the bottom of the old shaft from which the water had recently been removed, he told us within a few inches the exact distance from the last survey point to the bottom of the old shaft, which he had not seen for many a year. During these underground surveys we usually carried our dinner pails and ate lunch underground.

A new forty-stamp mill was commenced near the mouth of the vertical shaft, which encountered the vein some 3,700 feet from the outcrop. The vein of ore was later followed down for many hundreds of feet, until it crossed another vein from the other side of the valley. This was an unusually extensive producing quartz vein. The gold in the quartz did not occur continually throughout the vein, and sometimes very rich ore called specimen rock would be encountered. After any blasting at the face of the drift the first person to inspect the broken ore was the "specimen boss," who would pick up all the very rich rock; otherwise it would have been stolen. The high-grade ore was taken to the mine office and stored in the safe until the end of the month, when it would be run through the stamp mill. I often saw chunks of quartz as big as a man's fist that were fractured but could not be twisted apart because of wires and filaments of gold.

My work for several months was that of an inspector, to see that all building specifications for erection of the mill were followed. The new mill used steel and concrete, whereas only wood had been available for the first mill constructed near the original inclined shaft. I became intimately familiar with all the details of a stamp mill, which usually consisted of batteries of five heavy iron shoes that crushed the ore into small grains of sand. These flowed out over a copper table covered with mercury (quicksilver), which absorbed most of the free gold, while the remainder of the sand went over concentrating tables that removed heavy complex minerals. These were shipped to Selby smelter on San Francisco Bay. The last of the sand and slime was treated with a solution of cyanide of potassium, which dissolved gold that had escaped earlier entrapment. The roar of a stamp mill could be heard for a mile or more, and the men who worked in the building always stuffed cotton in their ears. Some became deaf.

After the high-grade ore was run through the mill, the copper plates in the mill would be scraped to recover all of the amalgam of quicksilver and gold, and the amalgam would be refined in the assayer's office. Ordinarily about forty thousand dollars in pure gold bullion was shipped each month by Wells Fargo from Grass Valley. No particular care was given to the gold brick. It was tied in a gunny sack and hauled to the express office in an open cart.

It was a great relief to me to have gone to a town like Grass Valley, which had been well established for more than half a century. It held many fine families and many daughters of marriageable age, and a number of young engineers found wives there. Such was my good fortune and also that of my friend, Edwin Oliver, who introduced me to Ethel May Kitts, who later became my wife. There were frequent dances in Grass Valley and Nevada City, and many families welcomed young people to their homes. One such home stands out clearly in my memory. Theodore Wilhelm, was was president of a small but profitable mining company, the Pennsylvania, very frequently opened his house to evening gatherings of young people and was a liberal host.

Among the interesting characters we had on the engineering staff at the North Star was a tall, handsome Italian who spoke perfect English with a decidedly British accent. I believe his mother was English. He had had university training in Europe and later attended the Columbia School of Mines in New York. His ambition was to have somebody point out a reasonably good prospect for a gold mine. He would do all the rest. I do not know whether he followed the mining business very long. He lightly told us that the nickname the boys had given him at college was "The Count." We assumed that he was a man of high lineage, but we did not know until several years later that he actually was a Prince. He accompanied Mussolini on his first march toward Rome, and during World War I he was in the Italian army in charge of artillery. One of his extraordinary feats was placing a gun on the face of a steep cliff that was almost inaccessible: he devised a scheme of lashing the gun onto the back of the strongest man he could find and then attaching several ropes to the man's body and having others hoist him up to the gun emplacement. Gelesio Caetani later became Italian ambassador to the United States.

He was an interesting conversationalist either at the dinner table or in the drafting room, and he often would put out some inquiry or make some remark that was entirely foreign to us. One day he asked, "Have you ever known a Russian?" When we all signified in the negative, he continued, "When you do, you will know the biggest liar in the world." Another time he asked the three of us if we were Catholics. When again we signified in the negative, he said, "That is strange. At home we are all Catholic; but we just raise hell with the Pope. It is a frequent saying at home that the faith of the people increases with distance from the Pope."

The town of Grass Valley had many Cornish families— "Cousin Jacks." Cornishmen had been hard-rock miners for many generations and suffered many hardships. Cornwall had supplied the world with tin for nearly two thousand years since the time of the Phoenicians, but a recent trip through Cornwall merely revealed heaps of broken rock and idle chimneys.

Cousin Jack miners migrated to various countries throughout the world where gold, silver and copper were being mined. They were expert miners and thoroughly accustomed to working under the supervision of well-trained engineers.

All the officials at the North Star mine showed me great courtesy and took occasion to help me in my chosen profession. Many Grass Valley men had gone to South Africa, where engineers and miners received very high salaries. One of them who was developing a gold mine in Rhodesia wrote a letter stating that he needed a mining engineer. My friends urged me to apply. Fortunately for me, nothing came of that offer.

Several years later I attended a Chautauqua performance at which a retired British civil servant presented a fine quartet of young African natives clad in leopard-skin robes. The next day I had an opportunity to talk to the man, and I told him how I had once looked forward to going to Rhodesia. He said, "Anyone would be foolish to leave California and go to Rhodesia." I asked him, "What are you going to do with the black man?" His answer was, "That is not the question. The problem is, what will he do with us."

A great many years later I became acquainted with Major Frederick Burnham, who risked his life in opening up the colony to white settlers, and I learned the complete details of that campaign.

Rhodesia's present status is now receiving worldwide attention, and the reader may be interested in books written by Major Burnham and John Hammond that cover the subject in great detail.[2]

After spending a year at the North Star mine, I decided to move on. Foote wrote in the letter of recommendation that I had been employed as "assistant engineer doing more or less of nearly everything to be done around a mine including mill construction in a very satisfactory manner."

---

[2] Frederick R. Burnham, *Scouting on Two Continents*, 1928; John Hays Hammond, *Autobiography*, 1935.

CHAPTER VII

Mining at Bodie, Manhattan, Tonopah and Goldfield

UPON LEAVING Grass Valley, I returned to San Francisco and began searching for an opening in mining operations. The general manager of a mine at Bodie, R. Gilman Brown, gave me an attentive hearing and shortly afterward employed me to make a comprehensive survey of the workings of Standard Consolidated Company, where my college friend Theodore Hoover was superintendent, and to take careful samples of all rock that might appear to be gold-bearing.

The journey required a night and a day by rail to the town of Hawthorn, Nevada, and then boarding a stagecoach of the old Concord type, such as are seen in western movies. It was so many years since I had lived in a cold climate that I made the mistake of wearing boots with hobnails in the soles. During the long night trip I thought my feet would freeze before we reached our destination more than eight thousand feet above sea level.

The driver of the stage was clad in traditional western garb— ten-gallon hat, long handlebar mustache, long coat with trousers stuffed into high black boots. He walked with an officious swagger. I made three trips with that same driver, once when coming down by daylight to Hawthorn seated between the driver and the Wells Fargo shotgun messenger, who had just brought in gold and silver coins and was charged with protecting the outgoing gold bullion.

We had an odd sort of economy in Bodie. The mining company paid all the employees in checks that were cashed by the local banker and Wells Fargo agent Jim Cain, with a discount of 1 per cent, which, he explained, reimbursed him for the cost of bringing the coin up.

"The Bad Man from Bodie" was the brainchild of a San Francisco newswriter. The catchword quickly spread throughout the West. Once when I was a little lad at my grandfather's ranch and I had been in some sort of mischief, my aunt said, "You had better behave or the Bad Man from Bodie will get you." Naturally I was curious to see the town.

The main street of Bodie was about a quarter of a mile long, with frame buildings on both sides except for two of brick. There were two hotels, three general stores and several saloons. There was also the fire house, headquarters of the volunteer fire department, which most of us joined because it exempted us from being called for jury duty at the county seat of Bridgeport and from paying the two-dollar annual poll tax.

All the buildings on the main street were destroyed by fire many years ago, and today the only buildings still standing and worthy of comment are the Miners Union Hall, the schoolhouse and one church. Many dwellings still remain in various degrees of upkeep or in utter ruin. A few years ago I walked into one of the ruined dwellings. The floor had caved in, and the remains of a piano had fallen through. Such sights always distress me, for I think of the hardships that families underwent whenever a boom town collapsed.

The town of Bodie is situated in a small valley surrounded by hills that are barren except for sagebrush. Not a single tree is visible except for a grove of aspens on the north side of a hill where a snowdrift remains until late spring and moistens the ground when it finally melts. All the hills are said to have been originally covered with piñon pines, which were all cut down, even the roots being dug up to provide fuel. A narrow-gauge railroad was built up from Mono Lake while the boom was still in force and continued to supply lumber and cordwood as long as the mine operated and the population stayed in the town. In the construction of the railroad many Chinese laborers were employed, and they were camped miles away from town to protect them from violence of white men.

Bodie had dwindled to about five hundred or a thousand inhabitants when I got there. They were hard-working and sober people. The miners worked ten hours a day every day in the year except for two holidays—Fourth of July and Christmas. The more skilled miners worked half the time by day and half the time by night, and their wages were four dollars a day, whereas at Grass Valley only three dollars was paid to skilled miners.

Bodie experienced a great boom during the early eighties, and mining men from the Comstock Lode at Virginia City, Nevada, rushed in, expecting to find an equally rich deposit of ore. Virginia City was undoubtedly the greatest mining camp in the West. It poured out a flood of silver that helped to finance the Union cause in the Civil War and build the city of San Francisco. The complete story of the Lode is admirably told by Lyman.[1]

At one time there were said to be thirty whistles blowing on the hill near Bodie where shafts were being sunk, with all sorts of skullduggery to extract money from potential buyers of stock. However, only two of the shafts penetrated rich ore, and that did not extend much below a depth of five hundred feet. The population of possibly ten thousand quickly shrank to about one thousand. The two productive mines were consolidated into one and continued for more than twenty years to furnish the livelihood of the small village, most of whose inhabitants were sober and industrious and some of whom sent their children away to college. The operation of the mine was continuously under the supervision of competent engineers, and many novel methods were introduced, one of which was the transmission of electric power for a distance of thirty miles.

The bad reputation of the booming new camp was caused by a large number of hoodlums who infested the saloons and gambling halls. There was the common remark, "A man for breakfast every day." Respectable members of society did not interfere with the activities of the hoodlums so long as their violence did not spread beyond their own circle. During my first year I listened to many arguments among old-timers over the

---

[1] George D. Lyman, *Saga of the Comstock Lode*, 1934.

exact chain of events at some shooting scrape or other. Hammond tells of shooting when he was in Bodie.[2] Only one conflict between the ruffians and the law-abiding citizens seems worth repeating.

The editor of the local paper, a Civil War veteran named Henry Z. Osborne, published an article that criticized the outrageous behavior of the rough characters. Thereupon a group of them came to his office and tore things apart. The next day a one-armed lawyer, who was always accompanied by an armed bodyguard and who had control of the Justice of Peace Court, walked into Osborne's office and made threats of what might happen if the editor continued his crusade. Osborne replied, "I know you are a killer. I am not. You could kill me if you wanted to, but it would be a bad mistake, because I am a newspaperman." Next day the same ruffians returned to the editor's office and repaired the damage. Osborne disposed of his paper before the boom crashed and moved to Los Angeles. There he was twice elected to Congress. The lawyer moved to San Francisco and established a profitable practice.

The cemetery of Bodie today is neat and well monumented, with no reference to violent deaths, quite in contrast to Boot Hill cemetery at Tombstone, Arizona, which has been jazzed up with ridiculous epitaphs as a tourist attraction. The cemetery at Bodie shows a high rate of mortality among young children. Doubtless many men died of pneumonia in tents or hovels during the winter months from the extreme cold and the high altitude. The thermometer falls below freezing almost every night of the year. One Fourth of July morning I saw a sheet of ice on the sidewalk. A fairly complete factual account of the early days of Bodie is on file at the Huntington Library, in San Marino.

My work underground at Bodie was quite different from the work I did at Grass Valley. The workings in the mine were perfectly dry, and the veins were comparatively thin, ranging from a foot to two or three inches. Little or no powder was used, because the rock was so soft it could be pried apart with what

---

[2] John Hays Hammond, *Autobiography*, 1935.

were called picker bars. The underground superintendent was an educated Cornishman named Bowdin who was very competent and succeeded in extracting considerable ore from pillars that had been left from earlier mining. He always provided me with a companion who was thoroughly skilled in the hazardous work of underground mining. I learned to avoid possible falling rock and bad air. The nearest I came to having a fatal accident was at Bodie. I was following the underground foreman who stepped on a pile of dirt at the top of a vertical shoot, and I followed. Apparently some of the dirt had fallen away, and there was only a slender bridge upon which I was walking. It gave way, and I fell about thirty feet, and my candle was extinguished. I was not hurt, but I was buried in dirt up to my knees. I relighted my candle and was pulled out by a rope.

There were several miles of old workings open, and I walked, climbed or crawled through all of them and took samples of whatever appeared to be gold-bearing ore. I was quite discouraged at the end, because I had found no worthwhile ore deposits, but Theodore Hoover assured me that he was quite satisfied: the manager and the superintendent were intent on leaving no good ore behind before they resigned. I traveled with Hoover to various parts of the county and examined mines, without finding worthwhile bodies of ore.

One summer I camped at an old hydraulic-mining cut that can be seen from Conway Summit on Highway 395. The work had evidently been carried on by people with little skill. They had dug two ditches to bring water to the hydraulic operations, but one of them was too slight a grade to carry the water, and another ditch had to be dug. I had a small crew of miners and a cook. When I lost one cook, another was sent to me. Neatly dressed, he carefully folded his coat and proudly showed me the certificate of an embalmer. Once he was recalled to Bodie to prepare the body of a man who had been killed by an accident in the stamp mill.

After about a year's work in Bodie I left to go to a booming mining camp in Nevada named Manhattan, not far from Tonopah. Both Tonopah and Goldfield were at that time actively producing gold and silver, but nobody knew that the final chapter of gold mining was being written. Goldfield was the last great discovery of gold in the United States.

From Hawthorn, I went by rail to Tonopah, where I visited a classmate of mine. Edmond North was the underground engineer of a very productive mine. He took me below, and we compared notes on the problems we had to face. He introduced me to the manager of the mine, by whom I was later employed in engineering. North lost his life a few years later in a mine accident in Mexico.

The principal producing mine in Tonopah was that of Tonopah Mining Company, which paid in dividends alone more than the total production of gold and silver in Bodie. I was offered a job with that company as an engineer but declined because I was bound for a booming mining camp. I was also offered a job as an engineer at the Copper Queen mine in Arizona, which I also declined.

When I arrived at Manhattan, the population numbered several thousand. Possibly a dozen or two frame buildings, tents and tent houses were scattered over the hills amid piñon pines and deep snow. Late one winter afternoon, with several inches of snow on the ground, I saw a most distressing sight—a middle-aged man and woman with several small children engaged in pitching tent beside a wagon and a team of horses. I have often wondered what could have become of them in that rapidly shifting and disappearing community.

The principal place of business in Manhattan, on the main street, was the Horseshoe Club, a large saloon and gambling house where many assembled because it was one of the few places in town where one could keep warm. There were all forms of gambling, and there was always the noisy drumming of the piano. To attract customers and to keep them as long as possible, the club ran an odd sort of lottery. Anybody who came in could register his name on the book, and at ten o'clock a winning name would be drawn for the prize of ten dollars. The registration was conducted by a dignified, well-dressed man who resembled a clergyman from some quiet country village.

Once or twice each evening a man would come in and proclaim in a loud voice that the bus was about to leave for the red-light district, a half mile down the canyon.

Shortly after I arrived at Manhattan, I made a preliminary inspection of the entire region, took samples of rock and crushed and panned them to ascertain the gold content. I concluded that the camp would never support more than a twenty-stamp mill. I wrote to my friend Theodore Hoover, who was about to leave Bodie for other operations. My prediction proved to be correct, and it demonstrated that I had served my apprenticeship as a mining engineer and was competent to evaluate gold-mining prospects.

The booms of both Tonopah and Goldfield, particularly Goldfield, attracted all sorts of people from all parts of the United States and from other countries. Young mining engineers from Boston Harbor to San Francisco Bay were represented in Manhattan, and every morning there would be parties of young engineers carrying transits and accompanied by axemen and chain carriers.

When I entered the camp, I found two of my associates from Encina, George Cromwell and James Dehy, and we shortly formed a partnership. Our work consisted mostly in surveying mining claims. We compiled a map of the district that we copyrighted, and doubtless any inquisitive person can find a copy of it on file in Washington. The jigsaw puzzle of overlapping and conflicting claims would have presented a fruitful source of income to lawyers and expert witnesses if rich ore had been discovered.

My Encina friend Jack Nourse was in Manhattan, and he opened a law office. We lived together in a tent for several months with only a wooden floor beneath half the tent. A sheet-iron stove served for meals but was no source of warmth. We went to bed early.

Jack once handled a lawsuit for me and my partners as we tried to obtain payment for the surveying of several claims. In later days he referred to that suit as one of the greatest experiences of his legal career. A man who claimed that he had been editor of a leading New York magazine was actively engaged in mining operations—that is, promoting any sort of deal that other people might pay for. He was one of the oddest characters I have ever seen. Short and stumpy, he wore high yellow boots and of course carried a prospector's pick. We had surveyed some claims for him, and he did not promptly pay us. Whenever I met him on the street, he would immediately tell me that within a few days his people at Goldfield would send him funds and he would reimburse us—all this before I had a chance to ask him for money. Finally one day I told him I was tired of the delays and was not going to stand for them any more. He replied, "If that is the way you feel about it, all right." He turned his back and walked away.

Our suit in the Justice Court was pure comedy. The judge denied our plea for reimbursement, and Jack said, "This only means we shall have to go some place where we can get an honest trial." As we walked out the door I remarked to Jack that he had taken a great risk of being fined for contempt of court. He replied, "The court had already adjourned, because the judge had stood up and put on his hat."

After a day or two the judge approached Jack and said he had been thinking things over and wondered if some further arrangement could be made—which, of course, he had no right to do, as he had already disposed of the case. Jack said that he did not care what the judge did, so long as we got our money. A day or two later another hearing was held; we got a judgment and received our money.

Once I was engaged in surveying and staking lots at a townsite called Stratford that never materialized. The promoters had a little camp some eight or ten miles away from the nearest water, which was brought in once a week along with groceries. The water was carried in whiskey barrels, and it can be imagined what a vile taste was caused by the few drops of liquor in the barrels of water, which soon became slimy and undrinkable.

One afternoon in April, after pleasant spring weather, I returned from the field and was told of a report that San Francisco had been struck by an earthquake and that people had scrambled out of Manhattan. The news from San Francisco was meager and conflicting, because the telegraph lines were either damaged or overcrowded. Sometimes it took three or four days to get information about friends or relatives in San Francisco. I was concerned over the welfare of my parents, who lived in Vallejo, at the northern end of San Francisco Bay. According to some reports, all of San Francisco had been swept into the ocean. After two or three days a report from Mare Island navy yard was on the wire, and I knew that my parents were safe.

Some six or eight months in Manhattan convinced me there was no use staying there, and I returned to Tonopah. There I was employed by a mining engineer named Mark B. Kerr to make a reconnaissance survey for a railroad that was to start at Mina and proceed westward to the sawmill on Mono Lake. The object of the project was to build a railroad and bring lumber to Tonopah. It all proved to be a business failure, and the road was never built.

The survey in the dead of winter, with two or three feet of snow on the ground, was a long, tiresome job. If it had been delayed a few months, it could have been completed with ease over rolling hills covered with sagebrush. After about six months of living in a tent, I had had my fill, and I persuaded an old Encina friend, Ralph McFadden, to take over.

One evening in early winter while I was still on the job, two Indians, a buck and a squaw, came into camp with one horse. Apparently the sudden snowfall had terminated their harvest of piñon nuts. We gave them a good warm meal, and they built a crude wall of sagebrush to protect them from the wind and bedded down for the night. When I left camp early next morning, I left word to give them breakfast and urge them to go on their way. When I returned, the cook said they had left. When I asked if the squaw was riding the horse, he answered, "Hell, no! She was walking ahead breaking the trail!"

I went to the town of Goldfield, where many lessees were operating on small areas of ground. The ore was rich, and much of it was stolen. It was said that in some of the leases there were more men working underground than appeared on the payroll, but the lessees did not care how much rich ore was stolen by the miners provided they got the maximum possible before the lease expired. The valuable claims were consolidated after the leases expired, being named Goldfield Consolidated.

I stayed in Goldfield several months with little or no objective other than to avoid camping in the snow. During my stay I saw the whole camp tied up by the Industrial Workers of the World, who proposed that every workingman from dishwasher to underground miner should receive the same pay. One day they tied up the town and held a parade. The next year the tyranny of the I.W.W. had been so heavy a threat that the state of Nevada, which had insufficient armed forces, called on the United States government to send in troops. About the same time similar trouble and anarchy occurred at Coeur d'Alene, Idaho, and United States troops had to be brought in. These conditions are vividly described in a book by Flora Cloman about her return to that camp as a bride.[3] Similar anarchy had prevailed at the mining camp of Cripple Creek, Colorado,[4] in which the state militia was called out to quell the riots. All these conditions prevailed some ten years before *Communist* became a dirty word in our vocabulary.

During my short stay in Goldfield there were some disturbances and shooting scrapes. One evening I was sitting in a cabin with several friends, when a burst of gunfire occurred nearby. We just sat still instead of venturing out to see who was doing the shooting.

I lived for some time in a shack that was owned by a friend and was erected on a lot in a new-found extension of the town. He was glad to waive rent just to preserve ownership. It shows the odd sort of people who were attracted to a gold rush. A man living in an adjoining shack had a Negro servant with him: what need he had for a servant I was never able to determine.

The following summer, after the reconnaissance survey, I was hired as manager of the sawmill at Mono Lake, the railroad and

[3] Flora Clement Cloman, *I'd Live It Over Again*, 1941.

[4] John Hays Hammond. *Autobiography*, 1935.

the lumber yard at Bodie. The few months I stayed on that job, I became acquainted with everyone in town, since they all had to buy firewood from us. I had a crew of Paiute Indians working on the upkeep of the railroad and lumber yard. They were faithful, industrious people, and I never had any trouble with any of them. At that time Indians were treated by most of the people as little better than dogs. One evening I went to a small camp of Indians near town to see if I could hire some of them. They were mostly young bucks and pretty well filled with liquor. Although I had a gun in my pocket, one of the bucks approached me with the look of a savage animal. I quickly retreated and made no further attempt at hiring.

One of the most fantastic characters I became acquainted with was Hank Blanchard, who is mentioned in Lyman's book.[5] He often came to my office, and we drove over most of Mono County in his buckboard. Once he said, "As a teamster at Virginia City my net monthly profit was thirty thousand dollars month in and month out. You may think that sounds like boasting, but when I tell you I left that camp broke, you may consider me to be a damned fool. You may take your choice." He told me how elections were conducted at Virginia City and how votes were bought. He knew from firsthand observation, for he stood at the polling place and watched the ballots deposited, and if it was a ticket he favored, he handed the man a five-dollar gold piece.

One day we were driving through a town, and he stopped the buckboard in front of the schoolhouse and said, "There are getting to be too damned many of them in this country. When a boy learns to read, he won't work." Some time later I learned that his principal ambition was to continue as chairman of the board of school trustees and that he was always careful to see that the very best teachers were hired.

Occasionally transient laborers came through Bodie and asked for jobs. A group came to my office late one afternoon, broke and hungry. I supplied them with food and blankets and

---

[5] George D. Lyman, *Saga of the Comstock Lode*, 1934.

put them to work in the lumber yard. They were best described by the old-time expression "the rag, tag and bobtail of hell." After a week or two they came to my office at midday and demanded their wages, which I promptly paid. The last I heard of them, they had spent several hours and dollars at a saloon near the outskirts of town and had started walking across the barren stretch of land toward Mono Lake.

CHAPTER VIII

Introduction to the Oil Industry

I LEFT BODIE in the middle of winter and returned to Vallejo. I was fortunate in obtaining a job as a subinspector in the Department of Yards and Docks at the navy yard. The interesting phase of that work was a survey of San Pablo Bay, which was very shallow and had to be dredged to take large vessels to the yard. I stood on the stern of a steam-driven launch, together with another engineer, with sextants in our hands, observing points on the shore in order to determine our position while the lead was being heaved from the bow.

While on that job I received a letter from an old Encina friend, W. Raleigh Hamilton, who had become chief geologist for Associated Oil Company with headquarters in San Francisco. The geological department of Associated was organized at the suggestion of Bernard Benfield, a civil engineer who had been a member of a committee that appraised the value of oil-producing properties that became the basis of the company. Hamilton told me they were putting on more geologists and that Professor J. P. Smith of Stanford was selecting the crew. I worked for that company four or five years.

I was given an introductory view of the country south of Coalinga, where the outcropping strata could be readily identified and mapped. My guide was Roy Ferguson, an excellent geologist, who, in addition to his habit of gathering pertinent facts, had an active and penetrating imagination. I well remember that when we stood on the crest of Kettleman Hills, he said, "I predict that the first productive well to be drilled here will strip the derrick." The geological evidence showed clearly that any oil which might underlie the hills would be found at such great depth that no drilling tools then in use could penetrate the oil-bearing strata. Ferguson's prediction was fulfilled several years later when Seaboard Oil Company drilled a well that came in wild and flowed out of control for a long time.

After my preliminary trips with Ferguson I began a reconnaissance survey of the west side of San Joaquin Valley. The survey continued for several months, and I traveled in a light wagon with a companion who served as cook and helped to pitch camp. No inviting oil prospects were noted except one in the neighborhood of New Indria, where a quicksilver mine had been operating for many years before Americans arrived in California and where many inhabitants were Mexicans who could not speak English.

Near the town of Altamont I saw one of the first rotary drilling rigs introduced in California. The men in charge of operations were Cyrus Bell and L. B. Little, employed by Standard Oil Company. They later played active and important parts in the oil industry.

After several months of field work I was assigned to a permanent station at Coalinga, and there I brought my bride, a second-generation native daughter of California. She and her mother were born in the same house in Grass Valley. My wife's grandparents were pioneers in California. Her maternal grandfather, E. A. Tompkins, was a physician who came overland from Trumansburg, New York, and arrived at Hangtown, now called Placerville, on September 20, 1850. A copy of his diary of the trip is on file at Huntington Library, San Marino. He served as assistant surgeon for two years with the Fourth Infantry, California Volunteers, during the Civil War. Her paternal grandfather, James Kitts, served one year in Company K, Fourth Regiment, Indiana Volunteers, during the war with Mexico, until July 20, 1848. A year later he led a wagon train to California and engaged in placer mining on a claim adjoining that of George Hearst, father of William Randolph Hearst.

Our first home was a three-room shack where it was not necessary to use a dustpan in sweeping the floor because the boards were spaced about a quarter inch apart and the dirt would drop right through. The only fuel we had was remnants of oil-field lumber that had to be chopped up. Our drinking water came from a barrel beside the kitchen door, after having been transported by rail some thirty miles. Most of the drilling crews and their families lived on the Associated lease in what was called Rag Town, a collection to tent houses.

When I first went to Coalinga, it was a firmly established town to which a branch railroad line had long before been constructed for the purpose of transporting a poor grade of coal that had been discovered in strata underlying those that later yielded vast quantities of oil. When my bride stepped off the train, her first view of the town was Whiskey Row, a block of frame buildings that were mostly saloons. In one of them was a short-order restaurant where you could get dry cereal and broiled steak. I was delighted to find that I had married a girl who was an excellent cook.

When we moved to Taft, we were able to find better living accommodations, though there had been only one house in Taft when I first visited the locality a few years earlier. It had become a thriving, wide-open town, entirely oblivious of sin. One night we were awakened by someone banging on the kitchen door and demanding admittance. When I opened the door, I was confronted by a quarrelsome drunk who had confused his address. I simply kicked him down the steps. When I turned to re-enter the kitchen, I met my wife carrying my six-gun, which she promptly returned to the holster hanging near our bed. There was no further disturbance.

Taft was situated near the base of Spellacy Hill, named for a prosperous oil operator who once was fated to become the losing Democratic candidate for the office of lieutenant governor when Hiram W. Johnson was entering the political arena. Tim Spellacy is credited with having said, "Half the lies told about the Irish are not true."

I was given no definite instructions other than to collect well logs, draw cross sections and construct underground contour maps. This sort of operation afforded an excellent opportunity to observe drilling operations, which were carried on with tools that showed little improvement over those used by Colonel Drake when he drilled the first oil well in the United States. His tools are now on exhibit in a musuem at the well site in Pennsylvania.

The mining engineer who found himself suddenly thrust into an old, well-established and profitable industry of which he was completely ignorant assumed a dual personality, part geologist and part engineer. In other words, he was a half-breed. He found himself surrounded by practical men who were skilled in drilling wells with old-fashioned tools capable of reaching a depth of two thousand feet or more; and for more than half a century such men actually created the oil industry. The practical cable-tool driller has disappeared, and he deserves a full description.

The cable-tool driller sat on a high stool with a hardwood club called a "forgie stick" with which he struck the temper screw that lengthened the cable as the well became deeper. Above him the walking beam moved regularly up and down as the drill churned its way into the earth. Typically, he was a native-born American of better than average intelligence who was proud of the fact that he had learned his trade at some oil field not many hundred miles distant from where Colonel Drake had drilled and, at a depth of some sixty feet, rock oil had gushed forth. The oil had long been recognized by the Indians where it seeped from the ground, and they valued it for its medicinal qualities.

Most drillers had strong arms and shoulders, gained during their apprenticeship as tool dressers, who swung heavy sledges on red-hot drills and beat it into sharp form. If the driller happened to use tobacco, which he usually did, his favorite brand would be Mail Pouch, which did not have to be cut or bitten from a plug but could easily be transferred to the mouth without interfering with manipulation of the "forgie stick."

In front of the driller was the bull wheel, which reeled the cable in and out of the well. The practical men who came to California added the calf wheel, which lifted or lowered the casing in the comparatively soft California strata. The people who paid the driller's wages expected him to "make hole" rapidly, and he kept a written log that was primarily a record of how many feet he had drilled during his tour of duty.

The length of the temper screw, which paid out more cable to the drill, was five feet; and occasionally geologists who had "walked on the rocks" and observed and measured the various kinds of strata, which varied in thickness from a few feet to as much as a hundred, were puzzled to read a log that reported each of the various strata to be five feet thick.

The driller usually made some note of the sort of rock he had penetrated. Sometimes he identified the rock with considerable accuracy; but if he could not do that, he exercised his imagination.

The driller worked continuously twelve hours a day. The morning tour began at midnight and ended at noon, when the afternoon tour began. If the two drillers at a well were in harmony, the written log might tell a different story than if the men were not. The average wage of a driller was eight dollars a day. Many an old-timer would state that he had "drilled against" a certain other fellow. The term might mean that they had competed as a team desirous of establishing a good record; on the other hand, it might be interpreted as unfriendly rivalry.

From time to time the drill was hoisted out of the well and the bailer lowered to bring up mud and fragments of rock which were dumped into the sump hole. Probably the first time the driller ever saw a geologist was when the geologist was inspecting the contents of the sump hole, and so the fellow was thereupon referred to as a "mud smeller," a name that persisted for many years.

On the average the logs preserved enough information so that geologists had some clues as to the sort of rock the drill had encountered. Unfortunately, some drillers never used a steel tape, and the reported depth of the well might or might not be accurate. Logs of wells were kept secret, as if they were priceless.

When rotary tools came into use, it was even more difficult to determine what strata had been penetrated, because mud-laden fluid was pumped down through the drill pipe and out through the bit and then rose to the surface, and consequently the samples of rock might have come from anywhere.

When I moved to Taft I was provided with a Locomobile, an automobile of an early vintage that often developed failures in awkward locations, requiring the driver to walk miles for repairs. The average life of a tire was about five hundred miles. The engine was started by a crank, and on a dirt road with a high center a pick and shovel were necessary to dig a hole deep enough for the down stroke of the crank. The duties of my job were still vague, and such recommendations as I made, suggesting the acquisition of land, seemed to get nowhere.

I conceived the idea that I could improve the services of the State Mining Bureau if I got the position of State Mineralogist. State Senator W. F. Chandler of Fresno County, whom I knew quite well, and two of his sons who had lived in Encina introduced me to Governor Hiram W. Johnson and recommended me for the position. I had one conference with the Governor and was encouraged, although he made no commitment. The chief geologist of Associated Oil, learning of my move, obtained a considerable raise in salary for me, and I then called on Governor Johnson a second time and told him my situation. He listened attentively and said, "I would have liked nothing better than to see my son sitting as a secretary at the outside door. But you know that four years from now the old crowd may be back in power and undo everything that we have done."

Shortly afterward I concluded that the job with Associated Oil had no future, and I resigned. Less than a year later the company abolished its geological department.

CHAPTER IX

Service With the State Mining Bureau

AFTER RESIGNING from Associated, I opened an office in San Francisco as a consulting engineer and geologist. The duties of that work were not onerous, nor was the remuneration sufficient to pay taxes on my newly built residence at Redwood City and take care of the grocery bills incurred by a family that now included two children. I was glad to accept a position with the State Mining Bureau at its headquarters in the Ferry Building.

The man who was first appointed State Mineralogist proved to be incompetent and caused so much unfavorable publicity that Governor Johnson ordered him to resign. The man next appointed by the Governor was Fletcher M. Hamilton, and he invited me to join his staff. Hamilton was a mining engineer of about my age. He was a graduate of the University of California and a gentleman of very pleasing personality. He had several close friends who were members of the state legislature. He was most cooperative and gave me a nearly free hand to carry out many projects that I suggested.

I visited several parts of the state inspecting mining operations, and spent a month in Mono County. I had an experience while there that showed how suspicious Indians were of any white man with whom they were not well acquainted. I wanted to return to San Francisco over the Sierra Nevadas via Yosemite Valley. I wanted to get one of my former Indian employees, Pat Gregg, to accompany me as far as Yosemite and then go back with the horses. There were a number of Indians camping near the village of Mono Lake. I inquired among them as to the whereabouts of Pat. None of them knew him or had seen him. It happened that my old friend Sheriff Jim Dolan, who for many

years was assayer at Bodie, drove in, and I told him of my pre-
dicament. He laughed and said, "Those two kids you talked to
are Pat's two boys." Only a year or so later, Sheriff Dolan was
shot and killed by a criminal he was pursuing.

One of my friends in Bodie had said that Pat was a dangerous
Indian. I knew that he had once killed a white man and had
served a term in prison. From accounts I heard, I was of the
opinion that the white man got what was coming to him.

We went up the Tioga Grade from near Mono Lake; and
when we arrived at the summit, Pat started directly ahead on the
road toward Yosemite Valley. He had doubtless been on that
route many times, bartering with Indians camped in Yosemite
Valley, exchanging, among other things, piñon nuts for acorns.
I called Pat back and said I wanted to take a more southerly
course and see some of the beautiful scenery south of the valley.
I had a good map and knew where the trails went. We proceeded
about a quarter of a mile, and Pat said, "I feel like lost right
now." We camped out three nights and had little to talk about
except what we were going to cook for the next meal and where
the horses would be picketed.

Pat answered questions but did not volunteer any information. Once I asked Pat how long an Indian woman was sick after
giving birth to a baby. "Maybe one week, maybe two week,"
was the reply. I said that a man had told me that an Indian
woman could have a baby and get up and proceed on the trail.
His reply to that was, "He damn fool!"

A traveler on Highway 395 between Los Angeles and Reno
may, if he is attentive, read considerable of California's early
history written in solid rock. For many miles the highway proceeds through an unbroken expanse of rough, black tumbled rock
that once was molten lava.

The summit of the Sierra Nevadas is in places carved with
deep U-shaped canyons formed by glaciers which, when they
came to the lower elevation, melted and dropped their unsorted
load of all sizes of rocks. That was a comparatively recent geological occurrence, only about three million years ago.

As one drives along the western shore of Mono Lake, he

will observe a number of terraces several hundred feet above the present level of the lake. They are the shore lines of an ancient lake that once extended far into Nevada.

Far to the east of the highway, and probably not accessible by automobile, are many hieroglyphics carved on large rock faces. Archeologists tell us that the first Las Vegas gamblers lived in that locality about ten thousand years ago.

After camping out three nights, we reached Yosemite Valley at the top of Glacier Point and looked down almost vertically half a mile to the floor of the valley. Air photographs had not yet come into use, and it took a little time to accustom my eyes to what I was looking at, but finally I realized that it was tents and houses. No automobiles were allowed in the valley at that time. I left by old-fashioned Concord stage via Wawona, in a beautiful forest.

Yosemite Valley now has so many tourists that it is difficult to find a camping place. I took three Boy Scouts there several years ago, and we had trouble finding enough room to pitch two pup tents. The government encourages tourists to go to places other than Yosemite and Yellowstone National Park, but the valley is in my opinion the most beautiful spot in California and well worth anyone's time.

I often visited Professor J. P. Smith at Stanford, and when I told him that I was working with the Mining Bureau he suggested I conduct a complete survey of the oil industry of California, I reminded him that an excellent piece of work done by two Stanford men, Ralph Arnold and Harry Johnson, for the Geological Survey seemed to fully cover the subject. Smith said, "How many people do you think understand that stuff?"

I spent a year in the oil fields, assisted by C. A. Waring, a young Stanford graduate, and our observations were published in a book (Bulletin 69) of about five hundred pages, which was well received. I presented the book as my thesis and was granted an advanced engineering degree by Stanford. We had visited all the producing oil fields, which numbered about thirteen, and we described conditions in all twenty-three counties where the presence of oil had ever been reported.

Dr. James Perrin Smith, my professor of geology at Stanford, was a natural-born teacher who thoroughly understood boys and sympathized with them. J.P. influenced the lives of many men who rose to high positions in the oil industry throughout the United States. His specialty was the study of fossils, but as a member of a small faculty he had to teach several other subjects. One of them dealt with the mathematical structure of crystals, and many of the boys considered it to have no practical use. His answer was, "No one can hope to become a successful mining engineer unless he can master this subject in three months and then forget it in the next three months."

The statewide survey of the oil industry revealed that in many fields damage to oil-bearing strata was caused by infiltrating water that had not been properly excluded. Plans to correct this had been proposed in bills introduced in the legislature. The bills would have authorized the formation of districts that were each governed by a board of directors elected by oil producers within the district. All these bills were defeated by protests from many small operators who feared the domination of a few large corporations. Furthermore, the proposed legislation did not specify any definite standards of procedure to be followed by the directors of a district.

We of the Mining Bureau decided to formulate legislation to provide that before an operator could begin drilling, he must submit his plan of procedure to the State Oil and Gas Supervisor, who must be a technically trained geologist or engineer.

Our proposed legislation provided that the expense of administrating a conservation law would not be paid from the general fund of the state—that is, by all the taxpayers in the state—but would be paid by assessments levied on all oil producers in proportion to the amount of oil they produced. The oil operators would be required to file copies of their logs of wells and to report each month the amount of oil and water produced in each well.

Our purpose was to induce all the prominent oil operators to hire their own geologists, who would consult with the deputy supervisor as to the best method of drilling a well so as to exclude water from the oil sand. Such consultation would have the benefit of all logs in the vicinity that had been filed with the supervisor.

The first draft of the proposed law was offered for study and criticism to operators throughout the state. Finally the draft of a bill was submitted to the legislature. Senator F. S. Birdsall agreed to manage our bill and requested that either Hamilton or I should be present every day in case some question arose. I attended every session of the legislature, every day, until our bill was passed.

It proved to be a most interesting and educative experience. I met and talked to many of the legislators. One of them was an intelligent Negro from Los Angeles. That was not surprising, because California entered the Union as a free state ten years before the Civil War, and Negroes there have always enjoyed the same civil rights as all other citizens.

When we first presented our proposed conservation law to the legislature our purpose was confined to simply regulating the manner in which wells should be constructed so as to avoid damage and waste of the oil resources of the state. At that time a group of operators engaged solely in the production of crude oil wanted some sort of a law which would protect them against fluctuations in the price of oil paid by large companies who might purchase their output. We declined to become involved in that problem.

In later years there were three separate attempts to regulate the amount of crude oil which could be produced and offered to the marketing companies. Such regulation would have given only incidental recognition to the prime purpose of our proposed law and would have established boards consisting of several members who would be constantly subjected to political pressure exerted by the various marketing companies. All of these proposed laws were defeated by the people of California in either referendum or initiative election.

When the bill finally was passed by the legislature, it still required the signature of the Governor before it could become law. Governor Johnson had not committed himself either for or against the bill, and we anxiously awaited his decision. He signed the bill, and it became effective in August, 1915, and I was appointed by the State Mineralogist as the first State Oil and Gas Supervisor. That law has now been in effect for nearly half a century without change from its basic principles, although amendments have been made to meet new conditions in oil-well drilling as they developed.

Fletcher Hamilton and I called at the office of the Governor, assuming that according to political precedent, he might wish to suggest certain persons for employment. The Governor listened to us, and then said, "I don't care who you hire. You boys wanted this law enacted. Now go ahead and administer it." That was typical of his entire administration. He never tried to build a machine, but sought the cooperation of forward-looking men, regardless of political alignment.

Upon my appointment as Oil and Gas Supervisor, for a term of four years, I was free to choose my own deputies and set their salaries. All other employees of the bureau were subject to appointment in conformity with the newly organized Civil Service Commission. My first deputies included Roy N. Ferguson, Robert B. Moran, Chester Naramore and Matthew J. Kirwan. Within about two years after the conservation law was enacted, most of the deputy supervisors resigned when offered higher salaries elsewhere.

Matt Kirwan went to Japan for a year's service with Nippon Oil Company. Upon his return he entered the service of an important subsidiary of Cities Service Company and was eventually promoted to director of all their field operations in Oklahoma and Texas.

Chet Naramore went into the service of the Bureau of Mines, in Washington, as mentioned earlier. Bob Moran returned to private practice, with an office in Los Angeles, where he was successful in discovering and profitably developing several new oil fields. Much later, while returning from Peru by air, he recognized geological evidence of a potential oil field near the headwaters of the Amazon. After several years of effort and expense he developed the field as a producer.

"Ferg"—Ferguson—went to Poland for a year in government service. Upon his return he became engaged in private practice, and by careful geological observations in California obtained many profitable leases. One of his most spectacular discoveries was in Ventura County, where he traced the course of an anticline that plunged below the floor of the ocean. He obtained a lease for this from the state, and it proved to be highly productive and profitable.

Jimmy McGregor, [1] a promising assistant, who was reared at an army post in Arizona, was fatally stricken at Los Angeles during the terrible influenza epidemic of 1918.

Most of these men had been members of the geological department of Associated Oil Company.

The office of State Supervisor continued as a department of the Mining Bureau, in the Ferry Building. Later the bureau was divided into the Division of Oil and Gas (DOG) and the Division of Geology and Mining.

During the summer of 1916, I attended Citizens' Training Camp at Del Monte. It was a fine experience. Regular Army officers were in command; one of them was Lieutenant George C. Marshall. When war was declared in 1917, I undoubtedly could have entered Officers' Training Camp, but with a wife and two small children to support, I decided I could best serve California by not going to war. The experience proved useful to me later.

I became rather intimately acquainted with Governor Johnson. A brief, unbiased description of his administration is given by Melendy and Gilbert.[2] Their description of the man's personality is, however, necessarily mere generalization, and when they say that some people found Hiram Johnson a very difficult man to get along with, that is a gross understatement. Had the two writers been able to undertake the task of consulting the files of dozens of small newspapers scattered throughout Cali-

---

[1] J. G. Bourke, *On the Border With Crook*, 1962; Frederick R. Burnham, *Scouting on Two Continents*, 1928.

[2] H. B. Melendy and B. F. Gilbert, *The Governors of California*, 1965.

fornia, they would have found testimony to his mettle in the
form of his spoken reply to the editor of a paper of wide circula-
tion in southern California who had impugned the integrity of
his father. That speech was a masterly example of blistering
vituperation.

The writers recite the names of many laws passed during
Johnson's administration, though failing to tell of the ultimate
results. They say of him, *"He must rank as one of California's
greatest governors."* (Italics mine.) They quote a letter from
Governor Johnson to Harris Weinstock, March, 1918, as follows:

> I chose the particular path in life in which I now find my-
> self. I chose it when an earning capacity had opened for
> me that would have led, undoubtedly, to financial ease and
> comfort. I made my choice, knowing the difficulties that
> lay in my way and that there were many things I could
> not hope for if I continued in political activity. Having
> made my choice, I feel that I must not only take the ad-
> vantages, but without repining, must accept the dis-
> advantages.
>
> I'm returning to you, therefore, your $5,000 check.
> Your letter and your offer have a value for me that could
> never be measured by any amount financially, however
> great.

Their account of the difference between Governor Johnson
and his successor from southern California simplistically portrays
it as a mere disagreement between them. Actually the demand
that the Governor immediately resign after being elected United
States Senator marked a change in the political weather: many
stand-pat Republicans, particularly in southern California, had
for a long time been violently opposed to Hiram and were eager
to see him kicked upstairs and out of the way. The demand was
absurd for several reasons; first, the Senate was not expected to
convene until several months later, and second, the salary of a
California governor was $10,000 while that of a United States
senator was only $7,500—and Johnson would be eligible to re-
ceive his senatorial salary only at some unspecified future date.

Hiram W. Johnson entered public life a poor man and remained so until his death.

I hope that some competent writer will gather all the facts relative to the long service of Hiram W. Johnson in the United States Senate and that, after that task has been completed, he will publish a book: "let the chips fall where they may."

Hiram Johnson never displayed much eagerness in becoming President of the United States. Irvin Cobb interviewed Senator Johnson in his hotel room at the time of the convention that nominated Harding.[3] The only persons present were Johnson, his elder son and his wife. The telephone rang, and Mrs. Johnson answered. She told the Senator that the caller was Teddy Roosevelt, Jr., and she urged him to answer because Roosevelt was "a nice young man." Cobb kept his ears cocked as Hiram picked up the phone, but all he heard was: "No ... no ... no ... not in a million years!" And finally, "Yes." Cobb asked the Senator if he would tell what the question was that he replied yes to, and the Senator said, "He wanted to know if I understood what he was saying."

About that time I was in Texas and other oil-producing states to see what they were doing in the way of conservation. Making a few inquiries among prominent politicians, I found out what the Republican party of Texas consisted of *at that time*. I handed my card to one high-ranking Republican; he glanced at it and said merely, "Ho, ho. How much money do you people have?" When I said, "Very little," he said, "Well, you had better get busy, because the Wood people have plenty."

A good friend of mine, A. L. Weil, a capable lawyer who later became president of a large oil company, once told me about an interesting incident involving Governor Johnson. Weil was in the employ of Captain John Barneson, a shipping magnate who was also interested in the oil business. Barneson asked Weil to obtain an appointment for a certain man as a member of the State Harbor Commission. He said he did not care how Weil got the appointment, so long as he got it. Weil wrote a

[3] Irvin S. Cobb, *Exit Laughing*, 1941.

Central part of
Grass Valley

Grass Valley
(1904)

Manhatten, Nevada (1906)

Top: Stamp Mill
Bottom: Main Street, Buena Vista, Colorado

Park County
Court House

Mt. Yale, Buena Vista, Colorado

Parmelee Ranch (1885)

Mt. Silverheels (Landmark of South Park, Colorado)

Lake View Gusher near Maricupa, California
(Produced 125,000 barrels of oil the first day)

Top: Coalinga, California (1908)
Bottom: Locomobile (1910)

Fairplay, Colorado   (Placer diggings worked by Chinese miners, c. 1882)

Painted Rock   (San Luis Opispo County, California)

Stanford University (1909)

Transporting of Equipment (1909)

Encina Club (1902) Front row, eighth from left, Roy P. McLaughlin
(Courtesy, The Stanford Quad of 1903)

Encina Hall

James Perrin Smith
(Courtesy, Peter Van Valkenburgh)

Hiram W. Johnson
(Courtesy, McCurry Photo Co.)

State Oil and Gas Supervisor and Staff (1916)

letter to the Governor and got a prompt reply reading in part as follows: "Dear Al: You know I do not like Barneson and he does not like me, but I can think of nobody who is in a better position to make a recommendation for that position than Barneson."

He appointed the man!

I had only one occasion to ask a favor of Hiram Johnson after he became United States Senator. That was on the illness of my deputy Thomas Kirwan, who had served in the Navy and was stricken with tuberculosis and forced to enter a sanitarium, while his wife returned to her former profession of schoolteacher. I visited Kirwan frequently at the sanitarium, and each time asked if he had received the federal benefits due him as a veteran. Dismayed that no action had been taken on his claim, I wired Senator Johnson, outlining the entire case. I immediately got a reply by wire saying that the Veterans Administration could not find Kirwan's number. I obtained the number and again wired the Senator, and he immediately replied, "I shall be in touch with the Veterans Administration every day until this claim is settled." Shortly after, Kirwan received the money due him. Some months later Kirwan was buried at the Presidio of San Francisco with full military honors.

I called on Senator Johnson several times at his office in Washington. The last time, accompanied by my wife, I handed my card to the secretary, and in a matter of seconds the door of his private office opened. He strode forward with outstretched hands and exclaimed, "My! I am glad to see you again! You haven't changed a bit. I can still see you the first day you walked into my office."

Of the many laws that were passed during Governor Johnson's administration, two dealt with subjects I was thoroughly familiar with: Industrial Accident Insurance and the Industrial Accident Commission.

While I was working in the mines, if a man lost his life through accident all that his heirs received was full wages up to and including the day of his death. Workmen's Compensation Insurance corrected that evil. Before enactment of the law that established the Industrial Accident Commission, there were no regulations to protect workmen against hazards encountered in their employment. No guard rails were required around moving parts of machinery. An acquaintance of mine in the stamp mill at Bodie carelessly stepped through the belt that went from a small pulley on the motor to a much larger pulley operating the stamps, and he was instantly hurled to death. Such an accident would not have happened if the law had required installation of a guard rail. The subject of first aid was never mentioned; ridiculous as it may seem, the only medicine stored at the small field office of the North Star Mining Company was a demijohn of whiskey, locked in an iron chest to which only the underground superintendent had a key.

The oil and gas conservation law provided for the selection of state employees through the newly organized Civil Service Commission, which was encountering some difficulty in persuading all state departments to comply. When I wrote the conservation law, I provided that all employees below the rank of supervisor and deputy supervisor should be chosen through civil service examination. When I later appointed deputies, they were almost entirely from among employees who had entered the service through civil service examination.

I only once, many years later, had occasion to consult with any governor of California. The cause of that consultation was that that governor had arbitrarily discharged one employee of the Division of Gas and Oil and demoted another. Less than two minutes' conversation with him disclosed that he was a mere garden variety of politician who apparently had no knowledge of any such thing as civil service. I got no satisfaction from him. However, I called the matter to the attention of a number of important men in the oil industry. I do not know what action they took, but the Governor quickly saw the error of his ways. The men were reinstated.

The law of 1915 declared that the people of California had a proprietary interest in deposits of oil and gas, and the new law was designed to protect the deposits against physical waste.

No provision was made for the regulation of the amount of oil that might be produced.

Monthly detailed reports were regularly published by the Supervisor, and they described any actions that had been taken. Descriptions of certain mechanical operations were circulated to assist operators. In addition, we sometimes published accounts of entirely new procedures. The office of the Supervisor was, I believe, the first to publish photographs taken from an airplane for geological purposes. Copies of all these reports are on file in the Los Angeles Public Library, and in other large libraries as well.

In our administration of the oil and conservation law we never issued *orders;* we merely wrote out our *recommendations,* and at the end of each month we published the names of all the prominent oil companies and noted what percentage of our recommendations had been followed. Standard Oil Company of California was always near the bottom of the list.

The methods of field operations that the Division of Oil and Gas adopted were not new. One large company, Kern Trading & Oil Company, a subsidiary of Southern Pacific Railroad Company, had already been following similar methods, under the direction of E. T. Dumble, chief geologist for the railroad.

Our first goal was to prevail upon *all* the large operators to employ geologists or engineers to present plans for drilling new wells.

Besides K. T. & O., two other companies readily adhered to the new program. One was Shell Oil Company, of which B. H. Van der Linden was general manager in California. Van der Linden was an accomplished geologist. We had many intimate talks when he was under pressure from his superiors in Holland to surrender certain leases in Ventura County that he had acquired upon recommendation of his chief geologist, J. E. (Brick) Elliott, an Encina boy. Shortly after the surrender of the leases in question Associated Oil Company, after having again established a geological department, acquired them and drilled many highly productive wells.

Several years later Van der Linden introduced me to two young Dutch engineers at lunch and told them about the leases he had had to surrender. Then he explained that in order to retain one of the leases he had "resorted to mere animal cunning" and told his superiors that a certain lease was along a paved highway, and certainly they could not think of surrendering that. The explanation did not seem to have much meaning to the Dutchmen, but of course the mere proximity of a paved highway signified nothing as to the possible value of the land for oil.

It was essential that we should gain the cooperation of *all* the large oil companies. The first one approached was Associated Oil. R. P. Schwerin, president, was a graduate of the United States Naval Academy and had for many years been president of Pacific Steamship Company. He was a polished diplomat and a gentleman of the old school. In the course of a long life I have never received such courteous treatment as when I first met Schwerin. His uniformed chauffeur climbed the stairway to my office, escorted me to a limousine and drove us to the most exclusive club in San Francisco, at the summit of Nob Hill. After an elegant luncheon my host listened attentively to my story. When I had finished, he smiled graciously, chuckled and raised his hands as a final gesture of appreciation at my youthful enthusiasm. Then in a kindly manner he advised me simply to be patient. Many of the older men in the oil fields, having old-fashioned prejudices, he pointed out, would not live much longer, and the changes I advocated would gradually be adopted. So—*that was that!*

The next step was to write to the president of Southern Pacific Railroad, which had a controlling interest in Associated. In due time my letter to President William Sproule was answered by a telephone call from a member of his staff. He said that Mr. Sproule had received my letter and would be glad to meet me at either his office or my own. I readily agreed to go to his office, which was only one block distant, and the date was agreed on.

Sproule was formally polite. He motioned me to the central one of three chairs facing him across the table. The other two were already occupied. He spoke in concise sentences designed to gather facts quickly. "I have heard of you, and I am sorry to meet you under adverse circumstances; however, the two men about whom you are complaining are now seated beside you. I shall be glad to listen to your complaint." I replied that I had no complaint against either of the two gentlemen seated beside me—Dumble of Southern Pacific and M. A. D'Heur, manager of operations for K. T. & O. On the contrary, I continued, I had upheld their methods of operations as a model of excellence worthy of consideration by other companies. After a brief pause Sproule said, "I did not understand the reason for this meeting. You gentlemen may be excused," and he motioned to the two men seated beside me.

Next he gathered up a pile of letters from the head of the production department of Associated Oil and began reading them aloud. One letter said that the writer favored the use of geological methods and had actually placed a copy of a popular handbook of geology in the hands of each field superintendent with the request that he familiarize himself with its contents. The second letter consisted of an explanation and justification of certain field developments that had apparently not been successful. Sproule dropped the letter without finishing it and exclaimed, "Elk Hills, hell! What is it you want, anyhow?" I replied that all we wanted was for Associated to employ geologists who could understand what we were talking about. "All right. It will be done," was the reply, and the meeting ended.

In due time J. A. Taff was appointed chief geologist of Associated Oil, and he employed Joseph Jensen as his assistant to deal with developments in Southern California fields. Jensen at first had to endure the dictatorial attitude of a superior officer who was irascible and entirely ignorant of geology and engineering.

Jensen, besides his successful work with Associated, has devoted a great deal of attention to public affairs and served continuously as chairman of the board of directors of the Metropolitan Water District of Southern California, one of the largest water agencies in the world. He is a member of the Colorado River Board of California and has served on the board of direc-

tors of the Los Angeles Chamber of Commerce and as chairman
of its Water and Power Committee.

We were particularly anxious to gain the cooperation of
Standard Oil Company of California because of its nationwide
reputation as a most efficient corporation. Standard Oil Company,
however, before dissolution of the trust in 1911, had never been
active in crude-oil producing, and Standard Oil Company of California began operation in comparatively new territory, where it
was not familiar with geological conditions.

My personal relations with the management of Standard Oil
were always pleasant. I was invited to lunch by the company's
foremost scientific adviser, E. A. (Doc) Starke, and learned two
things. First was my introduction to a beverage new to me, which
he called an "old-fashioned." Previously I had never believed that
bourbon whiskey could be relished when diluted with water and
sweetened with sugar. I still hold that belief. After the luncheon
my host gave me some fatherly advice, about as follows: "This
theory of water-bearing sands and oil-bearing sands which might
become intermingled is entirely false. I have demonstrated that
to the satisfaction of our people. You may dismiss it from your
mind." Doc Starke's erroneous statement regarding the inter-
mingling of the sands was an indication that we had a long uphill journey ahead of us in dealing with Standard Oil. Actually,
it required three years before we made the grade. The week
after our luncheon I returned the courtesy and had Doc Starke
as my guest. Our friendly relations continued for many years.
Despite his unorthodox notions of geology, Doc Starke discovered
several productive oil fields, and best of all, found jobs for
several young geologists, some of whom rose to the top. Frank
A. Morgan eventually became chief geologist of Richfield Oil
Corporation and was elected president of the American Association of Petroleum Geologists.

I was invited by F. H. Hillman, director of Standard Oil
Company of California and in charge of all oil-field production
operations, to call at its local field office in Whittier, where he
diplomatically introduced me to his employees as "your new

boss." Later I became well acquainted with Hillman and found him to be one of the finest gentlemen I had ever met, with the highest of ethical standards.

The high spot in my experience as Supervisor occurred one morning when I was on the night train bound for Bakersfield and then Taft, where I was to inspect completion of a well that my deputy had informed me was approaching critical depth. I raised the shade in my Pullman berth and saw on the horizon some twenty miles away a gas well afire on Elk Hills. I immediately knew that we had finally been provided with a demonstration that would impress the management of Standard Oil! The story leading up to the burning well is briefly as follows:

The company had once before proposed to drill a well in Elk Hills, and in accordance with a study made by Roy Ferguson, we recommended that casing be landed at a considerable depth above where they expected to encounter oil. Ferguson's study of abandoned wells in that locality had proved the existence of a gas-bearing zone above the oil-bearing strata. Standard paid no heed to our recommendations but were able, by some chance, to drill through the gas-bearing zone without recognizing its existence, and completed a very productive oil well. The company then proposed to drill a second well in much the same manner as the first. Ordinarily I left final decisions to the field deputy, but in this case I presided at a meeting with the company's field men. We insisted that a second well should land above the gas zone to protect it. But the state law lacked teeth to enforce our recommendations, and after a vehement discussion we were forced to accede, with their promise that a third well would be drilled in accordance with our recommendations. The manager of production, whose previous experience had been the laying of pipelines a few feet below the surface of the earth, assured me in no uncertain terms that Standard Oil Company knew how to drill wells and that after completion of the second well as they proposed they would drill the third "any damned way" I asked. It was the second well, drilled in accordance with

Standard's own plans, I saw on fire. All the facts, accompanied by a photograph of the burning well, were published in our monthly bulletin of May, 1919.

A few months later Hillman came to my office and thanked me for the consideration we had shown in our publication. He told me that it had required several weeks to extinguish the fire and that it had cost the company about seventy thousand dollars to repair the well. They were supplying gas to Los Angeles from that well, and with oncoming winter he hoped that nothing would happen to reduce their gas output.

Standard promptly changed its procedure and placed Reginald A. Stoner, a graduate in geology of the University of California, in charge of all field operations. Several years later he became a director of the corporation in charge of oil production throughout the world. He once told me that he would never have gained that position had it not been for the State Mining Bureau.

I last saw Reg at a barbecue given by Petroleum Production Pioneers, while I was in the midst of a political campaign. He greeted me with a term of endearment that is well understood among oil men and rescued me from instant political death by briskly pushing me out of a group of his fellow employees of Standard Oil who were about to be photographed. "Don't get your face in this picture," he said.

The one outfit that we were unable to convince in drilling methods was the group of "practical" men in charge of drilling for Union Oil Company of California. Having convinced all other companies that our plans were correct, we decided to try out the law to see how enforceable it was. We never had a "Chinaman's chance," because the group of commissioners who would act as arbitrators were all "practical" oil men. Our attorney at the so-called trial was Hiram W. Johnson, Jr. We were thoroughly and completely defeated. However, we published the facts in our monthly bulletin and showed how the property had been damaged. Doubtless that information came to the attention of the general manager of Union Oil, and they solved the problem in a very satisfactory manner, as will be described later.

While World War I was in progress, it was difficult for us to find competent young engineers, since most of them were in the service. When the war ended, several young engineers came to the Mining Bureau and applied for and received jobs. I met one or two former employees wandering aimlessly on the street. I told them to go to the Ferry Building and get on the payroll. "I don't care a damn what you *do*," I told them. Of course, there was plenty for them to do—studying maps and logs and becoming familiar with procedure of the department. Finally I had about half a dozen recruits. When I first walked into the room where they were seated around a table, they all stood up, military style. I waved them down, and no such performance was ever repeated again! In fact, whenever I visited our field offices, I made a practice of becoming personally acquainted with all new employees. As a consequence I always had the loyal support of competent young men who were eager to advance themselves in their chosen profession of engineering.

Another difficulty we had in retaining engineers came from the fact that the oil companies astutely saw the advantage of having such men on their payroll and hired them away from us after they had had a year or more experience. In other words, we were practically running a training school for the private companies.

Upon my resignation as State Oil and Gas Supervisor, about two years before the expiration of my second term of office, Roy E. Collum assumed the position. Later, R. D. Bush became Supervisor. Both of them were early members of my staff.

CHAPTER X

Business Ventures and
Managing an Oil Company

AFTER I RESIGNED from the Mining Bureau, I opened an office in San Francisco as a consulting engineer. It was more profitable than the job I had had with the Mining Bureau.

I became interested in a matter at Stanford University that concerned Professor J. P. Smith. He had been acting head of the Department of Geology but was superseded by another man without the courtesy of being consulted by the president of the university. He first knew of it through a newspaper. Such tactlessness in the president aroused the anger of many of J.P.'s former students, and we formed a committee to deal with the situation. I was appointed secretary. We decided to collect a fund for J.P. Both Herbert Hoover and his brother, Theodore, were generous contributors. When collection of the fund was completed, I visited the president of the university and told him what we had done, what we proposed to do and why we were doing it. About a week later we held a barbecue on the campus that was attended by many alumni and students. We handed J.P. a bankbook showing a balance of about ten thousand dollars.

We gave wide publicity to the affair, and the publicity went much further than we realized. A year or so later a visiting geologist exclaimed upon hearing J.P.'s name, "Oh, that's the chap to whom the students made a present of two thousand pounds!"

My friend Brick Elliott was organizing a company to drill a well near Santa Fe Springs. He had worked out the geology completely, and I was able to participate in the venture. The well produced oil in large amounts for several months, and we received 100 per cent monthly dividends.

I decided to move to Southern California, where a great boom in oil had begun. Wells were drilled broadcast, sometimes only a few feet apart, on town lots, and the wealth that gushed forth far exceeded that produced by the famous Comstock Lode.

That oil boom was an uproarious affair. A man named C. C. Julian promoted a variety of schemes, until finally his house of cards collapsed, and he left one bank holding a large bundle of practically worthless bonds. What attracted my attention to Julian was his flamboyant advertisements, which resembled the pitches outside a circus side show. It was reported that his "literature" was written by the same man we had once had to sue in the booming camp of Manhattan to collect a bill of two hundred dollars.

Among the many interesting and important men I became acquainted with was Henry L. Doherty, who in my opinion contributed more to the conservation of oil and gas and the furthering of engineering procedure than any other man in the United States. He was in Los Angeles with many of his engineering staff at a convention of the American Petroleum Institute, whose leaders had recently rebuffed him in his efforts to convince them that it was necessary to preserve the pressure of gas underground while it was still dissolved in the oil. He was familiar with what we had accomplished in California and asked me to conduct him around some of the oil fields and tell him of our problems. One of the most spectacular fields at that time was Signal Hill near Long Beach, where many wells had been drilled on such small tracts of land as town lots and where wooden derricks covered the hill like a forest. We spent an entire day together, having sandwiches for lunch, and as we drove back to Los Angeles he exclaimed: "This is the best day I have spent for a long time. Nobody knows where I am, and nobody can reach me by telephone!"

During his campaign to preserve gas pressure he had been denounced by some of the head men of the largest oil companies, and they had gone so far as to demand that he resign his position as a director of the API. His reply was, "To hell with you. I am not beholden to any of you fellows, and you have no more right to demand my resignation than I have to demand yours." He kept up his campaign, and within two years one of his severest critics stated publicly, "On a clear day Henry L. Doherty can see twenty years into the future."

Doherty's formal education did not go beyond grammer school, but he had a keen and inquiring mind. He organized the Cities Service Company, which supplied gas to many large communities. At his headquarters in Denver he had an experimental laboratory in a penthouse above the office building where he spent considerable time. One morning the janitor found the laboratory in great disarray and remarked, "The old man must have been working here last night."

Doherty told me that he had stumbled into the oil business when he was drilling a well in Oklahoma for gas and the well came in as a gusher of oil instead.

I once visited Doherty at Battle Creek, where he was confined in a sanitarium with painful arthritis, from which he never fully recovered. I last saw him in New York during an annual meeting of the American Institute of Mining Engineers. He was propped up in a wheel chair when he came on stage to receive the Anthony Lucas Medal, the highest award bestowed by the institute.

I never applied for a state license to practice as an engineer, but I participated in various allied business ventures, most of which were fairly profitable. During the depression, when everything was tied up and I had two children in college, I made ends meet by selling life insurance part of the time, while the banks were closed.

I once appeared as an expert witness on behalf of the state of California in a case where a group of "rugged individualists" had drilled wells near the shore and slanted them out under the ocean into ground that belonged to the state. The judge who sat was up for re-election in the near future. The growling and grumbling of the individualists reminded me of a saloon brawl;

yet the judge did not preserve order. The Assistant Attorney General telephoned to his superior, and another judge, from San Diego, was put in charge. The case established the fact that the state owned the land under the ocean; and laws were passed that provided for leases for such wells. Hundreds of them have been pushed out under the ocean floor along the California coast.

I once was chairman of an arbitration committee that was to decide how much oil each of several companies in Kettleman Hills should be allowed to produce. Part of the land belonged to the United States government. I conferred with a representative of the Department of the Interior, and he advised me to let everybody talk as much as I pleased.

In the short space of ten years the oil industry had become thoroughly science-minded. Among those who presented the case to us by talks and documents were engineers, geologists and other scientists. We conducted the hearings not by law-court procedure but rather as a discussion among scientists. We announced that each person would be allowed to speak twice, with no cross-examinations. Of course, lawyers of all of the companies were present and spoke, but we did not think lawyers knew much about how much oil the companies should produce.

Finally, after several days of hearing arguments, we went into executive session and studied all the documents and diagrams. The other two members of the committee were William N. Lacey, professor of chemical engineering at Cal Tech, with wide experience in the behavior of gas and oil under heavy pressure, and Walker S. Clute, a consulting geologist. Finally Lacey said, "There just isn't any answer to it," and I agreed. We did what any arbitration committee does. We figured out approximately what minimums the claimants would stand for and gave a schedule of the amount allotted to each of them. We tacked on a "formula" by which we had reached our determination. It was composed of scraps of all the varied information we had received. Since then I have been better able to understand why members of the United States Supreme Court occasionally write explanations of their decisions.

The first great improvement in drilling oil wells in such a

manner that the geologists could determine what formations had been penetrated was an invention of Brick Elliott's. It was a core barrel that would extract the core of formations penetrated so that geologists could inspect each and every stratum and could also take samples for microscopic examination of fossils.

The advance in the science of geology and in the art of petroleum engineering has been so great that I can only vaguely comprehend some of the discussions among engineers and geologists today.

A friend of mine put me in touch with a director of an oil company whose office was in New York. I was invited to come and discuss the possibility of taking a position with the company. I decided to try the new mode of transportation, flying. I spent twenty-four hours in constant flight between Los Angeles and New York, with my ears stuffed with cotton. Afterward, I made many trips to New York, always by rail. After my first trip I returned to Los Angeles with the title of general manager of the Burnham Exploration Company. I remained in that position for five or six years. It was one of the pleasantest jobs I ever held. The company was very prosperous, and my work was full of interest and romance.

About fourteen miles from the courthouse in the center of Los Angeles was a low range of hills called the Dominguez Hills. Most of the land was merely pasture land, and the top of the hills was nearly level. In the early days of demonstrating airplanes, the hilltop served as a runway, and great crowds of spectators came to see planes take to the air. The tract of land on which the Burnham Exploration Company started operations was a small portion of an enormously large grant given in 1784 by King Charles III to Sarjento Juan José Dominguez, Spanish Colonial Army (retired).

The range of hills was not notable in appearance, but a young mining engineer named Roderick Burnham, a graduate of the Michigan School of Mines, became interested and visited the hills many times. The board of directors of Union Oil Company, by whom he was employed, were lukewarm to his suggestion that oil might be found beneath the hills. He visited the field so many times, returning with foxtail in his trousers, that the men began calling him "Dominguez."

As a young lad Rod Burnham had panned fragments of gold jewelry from a water course in Rhodesia near an abandoned gold mine, of which there is no historical record, and it has been suggested the abandoned mine may have been one source of the gold of Ophir that the Queen of Sheba presented to King Solomon.[1] He performed important engineering work at the Ruth Mine near Ely, Nevada, and was leader of a crew of Union Oil Company geologists in South America. Also, he discovered for the Union Oil Company a highly productive field near Fort Collins in Colorado, and he conducted a sampling of oil-shale land that the company owned in western Colorado.

Union Oil Company did not choose to take leases on Dominguez Hills, so Rod asked permission to bring the matter to the attention of his father, Major Frederick R. Burnham, D.S.O., who headed a small syndicate working on a meager monthly allowance to find some profitable oil investments. Permission was granted, and Major Burnham, with the assistance of his South African friend John Hays Hammond, raised sufficient capital to proceed.

Not only was a zone of oil-producing sand found, but there were five of them, one beneath the other, interspersed with water-bearing sand and crossed by numerous faults. The area of the producing field was about a mile wide and two miles long.

When I became general manager of Burnham Exploration Company, whose name was later changed to Dominguez Oil Fields Company, I made a general survey of the situation and found that Major Burnham had been fortunate at the start of operations in obtaining the services of a competent young accountant named E. J. Leabow. The board of directors showed their continued good sense by retaining him until the company was finally liquidated. I am sure that the shareholders received every penny due them.

Union Oil Company became interested after Burnham Ex-

---

[1] John Hays Hammond, *Autobiography,* 1935.

ploration had taken the leases, and the two companies became partners, with Union being responsible for drilling and production. Shell Oil Company was another partner.

My most enjoyable experience during the years I was employed by Dominguez Oil was becoming well acquainted with A. C. Rubel, who preferred the nickname "Cy." He had spent about ten years as an engineer at the prolific Dominguez field, where he had been able to direct operations under strict engineering control. I was particularly interested in his achievement because of Union Oil's previous policy of ignoring such procedures.

The opportunity was first presented to Cy by E. W. Clark, executive vice-president and general manager of Union Oil, who had the reputation of making frequent unannounced visits to various operations under his immediate supervision, so that he would mingle with the men performing the actual operations. He apparently was a good judge of men.

I first met Mr. Clark at an informal meeting of important executives of oil companies. The meeting was at the San Francisco office of the State Mining Bureau and in response to our invitation. Our purpose was to explain our objectives. As one of the speakers I detailed some of our earlier experiences, including the statements of fact relative to the failure of several oil companies to understand our objectives and thus their failure to give us full cooperation. Among the companies mentioned was Union Oil Company of California. Clark was an attentive listener.

When he sent Cy Rubel to the Dominguez field, Clark was confronted with two vital problems: systematic development of the newly discovered field, which had great potentiality; and how to avoid creating discord among old-time employees who had loyally supported the company in several life-and-death struggles against being gobbled up by foreign interests. Those struggles receive extensive comments in the Preface of State Mining Bureau Bulletin No. 69, published in 1914.

After a general survey of conditions and a few brief conferences with Clark, Cy returned to the Dominguez field, and there he adopted a course that was really fantastic. He virtually assumed the role of an apprentice in the trade of "practical" drillers and actually worked as "a practical oil man." Any member of a drilling crew under a tall derrick risked physical danger like that encountered by men working underground in a mine.

Cy had previously experienced exposure to danger during World War I, to which he seldom referred. The most that I learned of it came from conversations with Desaix Myers, who had been his companion in a dugout when they received notice of their promotions in rank—Myers to major and Cy to captain. They were often under heavy fire from German artillery, and Myers told of leading his men across a road that was under shell fire. He said that he was thoroughly scared at seeing men literally blown to atoms but that his principal fear was that his men might see that he was scared. It was under such conditions that Cy was awarded the Distinguished Service Cross in France, as a member of the 304th Engineers, 79th Division. Inquiries as to that event were usually dismissed by Cy with some facetious remark.

One of Cy's early experiences at the Dominguez field, which he described to me humorously, was voluntarily accomplishing the hazardous operation of being lowered to the bottom of the cellar some twenty feet below the derrick floor where gas was escaping. He wore no gas mask but merely held his breath! The flow of gas could be checked only by human hands, which could close a valve.

We had several serious discussions involving problems in which the interests of our two companies were in direct conflict. Cy was endowed with a rare personality by which he could conduct negotiations without raising his voice or creating undue friction.

From the beginning of World War I many young engineers entered the service of various oil-producing corporations, and I observed their rate of advancement with more than casual interest, having retained membership in the American Institute of Mining, Metallurgical and Petroleum Engineers and in the American Association of Petroleum Geologists, whose meetings I often attended in various parts of the country. In total achievement, both as an engineer and as twice president of his company,

Albert Chatfield Rubel stood in the *first rank* and was awarded appropriate medals and honors. In addition, he gave unstintingly of his time and energy to public affairs, which in my opinion raised him head and shoulders above all the others. He was a trustee of Occidental College and of Southern California Orthopedic Hospital. He was a member of the executive committee of the Los Angeles Area of Boy Scouts of America and chairman of the Southern California Committee of the Freedoms Foundation at Valley Forge.

In politics Cy was extremely active in raising funds, and he contributed vitally to the election of Governor Ronald Reagan. He continued in that service by assisting Reagan in presenting competent assistants to various govermental departments.

In affairs of Los Angeles County he was a member of the Citizens Committee of Economy and Efficiency. In that capacity he was helpful in obtaining many useful changes of procedure. When he died, on June 1, 1967, at the age of seventy-two, all the flags at the county offices were flown at half mast.

My job with Dominguez was made more pleasant by my acquaintance with Major Burnham, who had received his military title in the British Army during World War I without losing his American citizenship. He was wounded and sent back to England on a ship carrying many high-ranking British officers and an irrepressible young lieutenant named Winston Churchill. He was decorated by King Edward with the Cross of the Distinguished Service Order. His book is a must for anyone who is interested in true-life adventure and history.[2]

No sooner had I met the Major than I found we had a common interest. He was an honorary member of the Boy Scouts of America, having known Lord Baden-Powell, originator of the scouting movement. I was at that time serving as a Scout Master.

Once I made a trip to New York with the Major, and I wanted to visit a Scout troop there. Headquarters told me that it was Saturday and I could not see a good troop. I told them that I just wanted to see a troop. I visited one in a settlement

---

[2] Frederick R. Burnham, *Scouting on Two Continents*, 1928.

house at the lower end of Manhattan Island. The boys, as I remember them, were all Jewish, and two young Jewish men came from the upper part of the island and conducted the meeting in fine style. None of the boys had a complete uniform; some had only a neckerchief or a jacket. But they were thoroughly imbued with the teaching of the Boy Scouts. When I returned to the hotel late that night, Major Burnham was sitting up waiting for me and told me about the troop.

Being a Scout Master was one of the most rewarding positions I ever held, although it paid no salary. It came to me quite by accident. Several of the neighborhood boys wanted to go to the Sierra Madre Mountains, about thirty miles distant, and try out their new homemade sleds in the freshly fallen snow. When we reached our destination, the snow was only about a foot deep and so light and powdery that the sleds could not go down the hill. I insisted that the boys tramp up and down the runway, until they finally got a few bumpy rides and were soaking wet to the waist and willing to call it quits.

We then went to a secluded spot at a lower elevation and built a roaring fire. The boys stripped off their clothing and hung it on manzanita and other bushes until it was dry. We got home in time for dinner, and no one even contracted a common cold. A week or so later I found that all the boys belonged to a Scout troop, and their fathers insisted that I become scoutmaster. My predecessor, Donald H. Fry, was perfectly willing to relinquish the position, having served many years. Fry had been the first boy to sleep in Encina Hall, before it was furnished. He walked four or five miles to it, and the first night had to sleep between two mattresses.

I served as scoutmaster for five years. Each summer we went to camp—not to a camp with every facility but in wide-open country several miles from Warner Hot Springs, in San Diego County. The accommodations were obtained with the assistance of my old-time partner George Cromwell. My short experience in Citizen's Training Camp served a good purpose, for I was able to show the boys how to arrange the camp, construct a latrine, pitch their tents in an orderly row, and how each patrol could cook meals over an open fire. I showed them how to gather up with bare hands the only substitute we could find for buffalo chips.

During our first season we had just broken camp and with packs on our backs were proceeding single-file to the truck that was to take us home, when at the head of the line an Eagle Scout sighted a rattlesnake. Without any ado he killed the snake with his staff, and we continued our hike.

I found that my principal service to Dominguez Oil Field Company was to constantly insist that Union drill more wells and produce oil more rapidly, and I was successful. In six years, beginning in 1934, they drilled 143 wells, and production was increased from about 100 million barrels annually to nearly 200 million. Dividends paid by Dominguez in 1934 were $820,000 and during the next five years they varied from a minimum of $1,020,000 to a maximum of $1,800,000.

While I was with Burnham Exploration, I became acquainted with W. W. Orcutt, who may be considered the dean of California petroleum geologists. He had lived in Encina Hall and been a member of the first football team to play against California. Herbert Hoover was manager of that team.[3] I was particularly curious to learn from Orcutt the details of a report that a considerable amount of liquor had mysteriously disappeared from Encina Hall.

When Senator Stanford and his wife founded Stanford University, some of the Senator's associates merely considered it a sort of hobby, like his breeding of race horses. A leading San Francisco newspaper declared that California had no more need of two universities than Switzerland had for a navy. To overcome the adverse publicity, the Senator and the faculty recruited students from various parts of the country. As part of his goodwill campaign he invited former President Benjamin Harrison, his friend, to come to the university and lecture on international law. At the first meeting everyone within driving distance was present, and space could not be found in even the largest room

---

[3] Herbert C. Hoover, *Memoirs*, 1951.

on the quadrangle. The lecture was given a second time, and Bill Orcutt signed up for the course. He said that at times Harrison showed up with quite a "sosh" and sometimes did not appear at all. The Encina boys deduced that there must be a store of liquor in the Hall. They got pass keys and searched various rooms, until finally they found the bottles, which had been given to Harrison by the Senator. They carried them up into the attic of Encina Hall, where the eaves hung down a full arm's length and there was room for the cache of two bottles between the rafters. There was quite a commotion about that loss of liquor, and a student committee was appointed to investigate; but of course it could determine nothing. The faculty was concerned, and to defray the cost of the liquor stationed some of their men at the Encina dining room to collect an assessment against each student. So far as I have learned, no more than $27.50 was collected. (It should be noted that the value of a dollar has since then dropped by 90 per cent.)

Orcutt was a remarkable man. He graduated from Stanford as a civil engineer, but in addition followed other courses of instruction, including geology, in which he attended all the lectures of Dr. J. C. Branner, former State Geologist of Arkansas, whom he accompanied on field trips.

When he entered the employ of Union Oil Company of California, which was the real pioneer in producing, refining and marketing petroleum, the company was faced with severe competition, especially from the Standard Oil trust. In searching for new oil deposits it was essential that their efforts should be concealed from competitors.

A casual examination of the range of hills south of the town of Santa Maria revealed to Bill Orcutt that the outcropping strata indicated the presence of a structure favorable for the accumulation of oil but that a thorough study and mapping of the region would be necessary before recommending the expenditure of money for the acquisition of leases and the drilling of a wildcat well. He chose to make such a survey in the guise of a hunter of wild game, and at the end of each day's work he would return to the local hotel with quail and rabbit for the cook. He told me that whenever he found an attractive prospect, he brought it directly to the attention of "the old man," meaning Lyman Steward, president of the company. In this instance Steward asked Orcutt whether the locality presented the possibility of a well capable of producing two hundred barrels of oil daily. Upon receiving an affirmative answer, he replied, "We can make a profit from such wells." Later drilling operations penetrated strata that in some instances held wells that produced several thousand barrels daily.

Several productive oil fields have been discovered in California without the services of geologists; Lost Hills and Belridge are examples. Many of the early geologists, including myself, inspected a seepage of oil at an inland valley of Santa Barbara County without realizing its significance. A young geologist named Thomas W. Dibblee, Jr., graduated from Stanford University thirty-four years after I received my degree, in 1902. He was soon employed by the California State Division of Mines, by Union Oil Company and then for five years by Richfield Oil Corporation. During his service with Richfield he spent many months carefully examining the geological conditions surrounding the aforementioned oil seepage and succeeded in solving the enigma to which earlier geologists had given only superficial attention. The final result was the discovery of the highly productive Cuyama oil field. The salary that Richfield paid that young geologist probably was one of the best investments it ever made.

CHAPTER XI

Retirement and a Fling at Politics

SHORTLY AFTER my retirement from Dominguez Oil, we entered World War II, and I made application to bureaus where I thought I might be of some assistance. Such an effort was entirely useless; I had reached the age of sixty-five and was therefore classified as obsolete. Finally, however, I received a long telegram asking if I would accept a position in Washington as an analyst. I did not know what they meant by the word "analyst" and had no intention of going to Washington to find out. Three short words would have been sufficient for reply; however, as the government was paying for the telegram, I replied at length, stating that I would accept any position for which I could qualify, provided it had to do with the winning of the war. Of course, I heard nothing further.

Like most people who are busy earning a living, I had taken little interest in politics. In 1914 when I was elected a member of the San Mateo County Central Committee of the Progressive Party, I remember that we had one or two congressmen from my district who could aptly be described as screwballs. We had for several terms elected a man who originally was registered as a Socialist but who with the advent of the New Deal quite logically switched his registration to Democrat. I was driving across our congressional district one day, which included such cities as Pomona, Whittier, Alhambra and South Pasadena—a prosperous country with oil wells, orange groves and several colleges—and I concluded that the people living in our district were certainly not Socialists. After discussion with a few of my friends I decided to run for Congress. I was gratified by the financial support I received from many associates in the oil industry. They contributed liberal amounts of money with no questions asked, although they were divided into three actively competitive groups.

For the first month or two it was practically a one-man campaign. I did not know what people had been interested as Republicans in the district and merely went around meeting editors. They were all glad to take money for advertising but were not particularly interested otherwise. Finally my candidacy was endorsed by Pro America, a patriotic women's group. The campaign immediately speeded up.

I knew that any candidate who expected to be elected must be certain of carrying his home precinct. The suburban town of South Pasadena knew little or nothing about me except possibly that I was a Scout Master, and I had no idea how the Republican politicians there would regard my candidacy. That was cleared up when my classmate Andrew J. Copp, Jr., appeared before the Republican Club and gave an enthusiastic complimentary account of my services under Governor Hiram Johnson. The club endorsed my candidacy.

I announced that I had two purposes in mind: first, to get elected; and second, of equal importance, to create harmony among all Republicans in the district. I did not achieve the first purpose and was not greatly disappointed. I had known that the odds were against me. My wife, who passed away ten years later, was greatly relieved when I told her that I would not run again, for she did not enjoy shaking long lines of hands.

I was, however, entirely successful in harmonizing the Republicans, and two years later several persons were anxious to run for Congress on the Republican ticket, whereas no one had previously cared to. We organized a "fact-finding committee" and interviewed all prospective candidates. We finally endorsed the candidacy of Richard M. Nixon, who was elected.[1]

After several months of political campaigning it was quite easy for me to settle down to a full-time job of retirement. I took up several hobbies, and I traveled in half a dozen foreign coun-

---

[1] Richard M. Nixon, *Six Crises*, 1962.

tries. A high spot was a reunion of my old Scout Troop at my home. The boys had all been in the Army, and they ranged from private to lieutenant colonel.

One of the boys, with poor eyesight, was disappointed that he had not got into active service but had merely been assigned to some supply depot to sort nuts and bolts. However, he did not lose his sense of humor: the boys were once given a trip to Catalina Island, and he applied for overseas pay.

One of the boys had been a tail gunner in a bomber over Germany. Another had served as a captain of artillery in Italy. The boy who rose to rank of lieutenant colonel had enlisted under some specious promise that if he enlisted promptly, he would serve only eighteen months. He took the promise at face value, got married and enlisted. As a matter of record, he served a full five years. I asked him where he had been during those five years, and he replied, "Oh, almost every place. The last two years I was shoving papers across MacArthur's desk."

Epilogue

How THE American people have acted since the beginning of our comparatively brief history is briefly and entertainingly related by Thomas A. Bailey.[1]

In ancient Greece a wealthy man started his son on a tour of the world with the admonition, "My son, as you travel observe with how little foresight human affairs are conducted."

Much later Winston Churchill declared, "Democracy is the worst form of government there is, with the exception of all others in existence."

The two great empires of Britain and Germany fought to the death, and the vacuum has been filled by two other groups of vigorous and intelligent people, the Russians and the Chinese, both experimenting with communist rule. An eminent Canadian scientist, John Tuzo Wilson, tells of his traveling with considerable freedom in several communist countries.[2] He tells how scientists of many countries, including Communist Russia, fully cooperated in scientific observations during the International Geophysical Year. He briefly states some of the results obtained from study of the earth and of outer space, from which we are continuously bombarded by a variety of rays, some of which probably affect the human race.

Professional soldiers in the United States do not encourage war, but on the contrary take steps to prevent it. "Politicians start wars and soldiers have to end them." The memoirs of General Ridgway, published several years before we landed troops in Vietnam, demonstrate the soldier's aim.[3] The survey of that country that he authorized clearly revealed the almost insurmountable obstacles presented in the Vietnam terrain.

---

[1] *The American Pageant*, 1956.

[2] *One Chinese Moon*, 1959; *The Year of the New Moons*, 1961.

[3] Matthew B. Ridgway, *Memoirs*, 1956, pp. 275-78

During the second half of our national history we have been engaged in five wars. Our population has increased less than four fold while our national debt has increased more than one hundred and sixty fold.

If the reader's interest has been sustained, I shall add to his content my own, with the recollection that I have always had my full share of the breaks of the game.